# How to Get Your Share of the $30-Plus Billion Being Offered by U.S. Foundations:

## A Complete Guide for Locating, Preparing, and Presenting Your Proposals

### By Richard Helweg

### Foreword by Debbie DiVirgilio

HOW TO GET YOUR SHARE OF THE $30-PLUS BILLION BEING OFFERED BY U.S. FOUNDATIONS: A COMPLETE GUIDE FOR LOCATING, PREPARING, AND PRESENTING YOUR PROPOSALS

Copyright © 2010 Atlantic Publishing Group, Inc.
1405 SW 6th Avenue • Ocala, Florida 34471 • Phone 800-814-1132 • Fax 352-622-1875
Web site: www.atlantic-pub.com • E-mail: sales@atlantic-pub.com
SAN Number: 268-1250

Library of Congress Cataloging-in-Publication Data

Helweg, Richard.
  How to get your share of the 30-plus billion dollars being offered by U.S. foundations : a complete guide for locating, preparing, and presenting your proposals / Richard Helweg.
    p. cm.
  Includes bibliographical references and index.
  ISBN-13: 978-1-60138-258-0 (alk. paper)
  ISBN-10: 1-60138-258-8 (alk. paper)
  1. Proposal writing for grants--United States. 2. Fund raising--United States. 3. Proposal writing for grants--United States--Case studies. 4. Fund raising--United States--Case studies.
I. Title.
  HG177.5.U6.H677 2009
  658.15'224--dc22
                        2008032592

Printed in the United States

PROJECT MANAGER: Carrie Speight
ASSISTANT EDITOR: Angela Pham • apham@atlantic-pub.com
COVER DESIGN: Jackie Miller • sullmill@charter.net
INTERIOR DESIGN: Samantha Martin • smartin@atlantic-pub.com

Printed on Recycled Paper

We recently lost our beloved pet "Bear," who was not only our best and dearest friend but also the "Vice President of Sunshine" here at Atlantic Publishing. He did not receive a salary but worked tirelessly 24 hours a day to please his parents. Bear was a rescue dog that turned around and showered myself, my wife, Sherri, his grandparents Jean, Bob, and Nancy, and every person and animal he met (maybe not rabbits) with friendship and love. He made a lot of people smile every day.

We wanted you to know that a portion of the profits of this book will be donated to The Humane Society of the United States.   *–Douglas & Sherri Brown*

---

The human-animal bond is as old as human history. We cherish our animal companions for their unconditional affection and acceptance. We feel a thrill when we glimpse wild creatures in their natural habitat or in our own backyard.

Unfortunately, the human-animal bond has at times been weakened. Humans have exploited some animal species to the point of extinction.

The Humane Society of the United States makes a difference in the lives of animals here at home and worldwide. The HSUS is dedicated to creating a world where our relationship with animals is guided by compassion. We seek a truly humane society in which animals are respected for their intrinsic value, and where the human-animal bond is strong.

Want to help animals? We have plenty of suggestions. Adopt a pet from a local shelter, join The Humane Society and be a part of our work to help companion animals and wildlife. You will be funding our educational, legislative, investigative and outreach projects in the U.S. and across the globe.

Or perhaps you'd like to make a memorial donation in honor of a pet, friend or relative? You can through our Kindred Spirits program. And if you'd like to contribute in a more structured way, our Planned Giving Office has suggestions about estate planning, annuities, and even gifts of stock that avoid capital gains taxes.

Maybe you have land that you would like to preserve as a lasting habitat for wildlife. Our Wildlife Land Trust can help you. Perhaps the land you want to share is a backyard— that's enough. Our Urban Wildlife Sanctuary Program will show you how to create a habitat for your wild neighbors.

So you see, it's easy to help animals. And The HSUS is here to help.

**THE HUMANE SOCIETY**
**OF THE UNITED STATES.**

**2100 L Street NW • Washington, DC 20037 • 202-452-1100**
**www.hsus.org**

# Dedication

*Thanks go to Karen, Aedan, and Rory for granting me time.*
*Thanks to Hilary for granting me direction.*

# Table of Contents

# Foreword

If your nonprofit organization is like most, the search for funding is never-ending. To meet this need for funding, many organizations seek grant funding, and, according to the information being published by many foundations, more organizations than ever are seeking grant funds. This process can be daunting, overwhelming, and time-consuming.

Richard Helweg, author of *How to Get Your Share of the $30-Plus Billion Being Offered by U.S. Foundations: A Complete Guide for Locating, Preparing, and Presenting Your Proposals*, offers a user-friendly guide for novice and experienced grant writers alike. While there are many books that will provide grant seekers with a guide to grant writing, this book goes beyond the basics.

Helweg first guides organizations through the development of a mission statement. Throughout, he stresses the importance of staying true to the mission and not chasing grant dollars, as so many organizations are apt to do in their search for funding. The book includes an overview of the types of funding available so grant-seekers can think about the types of grants that are best for their organization, and they can understand how to approach the funder.

The most important information in this book focuses on researching and linking the needs of your organization/community to the interests of potential funding sources. Once possible sources have been identified, it is time for the application process — which often begins with a letter of inquiry. In my experience, more foundations use the letter of inquiry process as the initial starting point for organizations seeking funding. This enables foundations to quickly assess those organizations that they are interested in learning more about.

Once initial contact has been made, it is time to write the actual grant proposal. Helweg goes step-by-step through the process for writing a successful proposal. He includes the post-proposal steps that so many grant seekers forget, including obtaining funds, not being funded, receiving partial funding, and, above all, being a good steward of grant funds.

As a grant writer for more than 20 years, I found the information contained within the book to be on-track with the advice that I give to my clients At least 75 percent of an organization's success in obtaining grant funding from foundations is due to the research that is done before anything is written. As Helweg emphasizes, an organization must carefully research potential funding sources to ensure the organization and the foundation are a good match. Putting time into research will reduce the amount of frustration experienced by the grant seeker while increasing the number of proposals that are funded.

Grant seekers will find it helpful to keep a copy of Helweg's book on their bookshelf to refer to the golden nuggets of information again and again. As you search for funding sources, remember that grant funding is not a quick fix. In the best-case scenario, it takes 6 to 9 months.

Do not get discouraged; there are many reasons proposals are not funded that the grant writer cannot control. Stick with it, and success will come. Best of luck as you work to obtain the funding to fulfill your organization's mission.

*Debbie DiVirgilio has more than 20 years experience in the non-profit sector, where she has been successful in obtaining foundation, state, and federal grant funding. She worked in a variety of nonprofit organizations before starting a non-profit consulting firm. The firm, DiVirgilio & Associates LLC, provides grant writing services for faith- and community-based organizations, public safety organizations, schools, and local governments. DiVirgilio has expertise in program development and holds a master's degree in nonprofit management. DiVirgilio is certified by the Grant Professional Certification Institute and serves on the board of directors for the American Association of Grant Professionals.*

# Introduction

Every year, U.S. foundations give away billions of dollars for everything from putting on dance programs to helping traffic congestion around elementary schools. To receive some of this money, you have to know your company and who is offering funding, as well as the proper procedures to follow.

The amount of money given away by foundations fluctuates every year depending on the state of the economy, but who the money is given to and why remains fairly steady. Foundations make grants available to organizations and individuals because they believe in their ability and purpose. A large pharmaceutical corporation might make grants available to students who go to school to study medicine. A retail chain might make grants available to organizations that work to improve the quality of life in communities where the chain has stores. In this sense, foundation grants are available from a huge number of foundations for an endless variety of purposes. The mission of this book is to help you identify who to ask and how to ask them.

Whether you are searching for funding to help your organization clean up the parks in your community, or you are an aspiring cartoonist looking for educational assistance, there is a good chance that grant money is available to help you realize your vision. You do not have to be an established not-for-profit organization to benefit from a foundation grant. But the ability to tell your story and share your vision is required. Our mission is to help you do that.

Much of this book is written from the perspective of a small not-for-profit organization in search of foundation grant dollars. But if you are an individual in search of grant funding, you can benefit from the lessons offered here just as much as that small organization.

This book will guide you from the first step in your quest for a foundation grant to the thank-you letter you will write after receiving a check for $25,000. We will help you search for a foundation grant, write an initial letter of inquiry, and write a clear and purposeful proposal.

This book is a practical guide to locating grants and preparing and presenting your foundation proposals, written for those who have never developed a funding proposal before. It will serve as an essential resource for the more seasoned grant seeker. Whether you are reading this from an organization's perspective or you are an individual in search of funding, you will find this book useful. The book is divided into three parts: *The Components of Your Grant, Writing the Proposal*, and *Now What?*

The first part, *The Components of Your Grant*, discusses ways to search for a foundation grant. *The Components of Your Grant* will describe all the elements of a grant request that you can prepare before even starting your search. More specifically, it will detail the information the grant seeker will have to prepare for their funding proposal. By ensuring that the seeker is prepared with the information described in this part, they will avoid staring at a "blank page," trying to figure out what to write.

The *Writing the Proposal* section covers the essentials of matching your written proposal to the guidelines offered by the particular foundations. The chapters in *Writing the Proposal* include numerous examples of cover letters, grant proposals, and thank-you letters.

Part three, *Now What?*, reviews various scenarios that may occur whether funding has been received or not. The chapters in *Now What?* examine the stewardship of foundation funding and what happens if funding is awarded, denied, or partially awarded.

If you are new to researching and writing foundation grant proposals, it is vital to start at the beginning. Schedule six weeks to work through the steps described in this book. If you find that you have already done much of the preparatory work described here, the schedule will be shorter. If you are a more seasoned seeker of foundation support, you may find the various sections and chapters useful as inspiration on a new, and perhaps different, way of approaching funders.

Some of the most important information you can find in this book can be found in the case studies. The advice given here comes from a cumulative total of more than 100 years of grant-seeking. The case studies come from a wide variety of sources that are located across the United States, from arts organizations, museums, conservation groups, and human service organizations. They present people who are professional grant writers, volunteer grant writers, development directors, and executive directors of not-for-profit organizations.

In this book, you will read the fictional story of Amicitia Gardens, a not-for-profit community garden created for this book to serve as an example of the funding process. Of the three foundations that Amicitia Gardens' Executive Director Rose Flowers pursues throughout the book, she will have the most success with the foundation that she has the closest relationship. Rose's story and actions will serve as a good example of what you should do during your foundation search and proposal.

When you talk to people about your organization, you must remember that what is important is not the fact that you are seeking funding, but that you have a mission. Your mission is not to raise money, but to assist families, neighborhoods, and organizations.

Another common thread you will find throughout these case studies is preparation. I have sat in on numerous committees that review grant applications and have found that most proposals are just not ready to attract money. Generally, the proposals are not complete; in addition, most have not taken advantage of collaborating with all their stakeholders and utilizing their network. This book, along with the input from many professionals in the case studies, will explain how important it is to follow grant guidelines and to network with people in your organization for connections that may prove to be useful in the search for funding.

A piece of advice that is quite common throughout these case studies is the careful consideration of your organizational needs. Before you spend the time and energy to pursue a funding proposal, make sure that the need goes beyond your organization. It is one thing to say your organization needs something, but it is quite different to say how meeting this need will affect more than just your organization; it will affect your community. Many experienced grant seekers will tell you that a compelling need addressed in a highly effective, innovative, and collaborative way makes for a forceful proposal. Too many organizations are doing the same thing, competing pointlessly with each other. When this is the case, the need is not as strong, and your case is not as compelling.

You will find this book to be a useful, practical guide. We will touch on every important point of the foundation grant. Take notes along the way; even write your grant proposal as you read. The more you engage in the process, the better at it you will become.

# PART ONE

## THE COMPONENTS OF YOUR GRANT

# Section 1

---

## Know Yourself (The Basics)

We deal here with the most basic elements of any foundation grant proposal. Before you do any research into what foundations are and what they support, you must have a firm grasp on what your organization stands for. The foundations will want to know what your mission is and will expect you to describe the vision of your organization. They want to know if you see the big picture, and if your organization's vision fits into the community at-large. They will also be interested in knowing about your organization's history. Because you are proposing that they provide you with funding, they will want to trust that the organization or individual is able to responsibly manage any funds they offer.

To ease your entry into the world of foundation grants, it is worth your while to prepare the information before sitting down to write your first grant. If you do this preparation, the writing of the grant will be a matter of pulling the required pieces together. Not every foundation will ask for every bit of information presented in this book, but having this information on hand for future grant writing will be useful.

# Chapter 1

## What is Your Mission?

*What is my purpose?* This heavy question may be the most important question you answer in your quest for a foundation grant. Being able to answer this question in a clear, concise manner tells funders that you are professional and understand your organization's goals. This is your mission statement.

Without a doubt, the most important part of any organizational request for foundation funding is the mission statement. Likewise, if you are an individual seeking funding, you must be able to state your business. A mission statement defines what your business is all about; a mission statement is your reason for being.

You should be able to define your mission in one simple sentence. It is well-worth your time and effort to work on your mission statement until it is perfect — that is, when it clearly and concisely defines your purpose. When someone can read it quickly and know what your business focus is without your needing to clarify it, add something to it, or answer any questions, your mission statement will be complete.

The importance of a mission statement can be compared to the importance of a plot in a good story. In literature, a writer might refer to the mission as the plot, or more simply, as an action. You recognize when you are reading a book or watching a movie with a good plot: If someone asks you what the story is about, you can explain it easily. Or think about the movies you have seen that have a poorly defined plot. The characters may be good; the movie may have been beautifully filmed. But if there is no plot, the movie fails. The same can be said about your funding proposal. If you cannot state what it is you do, the funders will pass you by.

## Grant Seeking Tip

To begin creating a strong mission statement, think in terms of active verbs. Your organization was formed to do something. If you are looking for funding as an individual, you are involved in some type of activity. Describe this activity using active verbs.

To assist you in learning about writing a foundation grant proposal we will start by creating a model that you can refer to when seeking and writing a proposal. We will use a community garden cooperative as our model, a fictional cooperative that will focus on growing vegetables, but can also grow herbs and flowers. Our community garden will be called Amicitia Community Gardens.

**"Amicitia Community Gardens is a community gardening cooperative with the mission to assist families, neighborhoods, and organizations in growing food for themselves and the community."**

The statement in bold is Amicitia Community Gardens' mission statement. Nothing else needs to be said; it is simple and to the point. The active verb in this mission is "to assist."

Their mission statement tells us that their group is a cooperative community garden, and that they help families, neighborhoods, and organizations grow food for themselves and their communities. Simple.

The biggest trap you can run into in creating a mission statement is to say too much. For example, "The mission of Amicitia Community Gardens is to create an environment in which the inhabitants of our community can claim a plot of land where they might grow vegetables for themselves to feed their family and enrich, nourish, and invigorate not only the community, but the planet as well." This sounds like the mission of a green theme park. From reading this mission, we feel that Amicitia Community Gardens is organized for a crusade to save the planet as opposed to "...assist[ing] families, neighborhoods, and organizations in growing food for themselves and their communities." In fact, the active verb has changed from "to assist" to "to create." If it is to be a community garden, "to assist" makes more sense than "to create." Their community garden may enrich, nourish, and invigorate the community and the planet, but this is incidental to the basic mission of the organization.

The basic rule for your mission statement is to keep it simple. The people reading your proposal are reading hundreds of other requests for funding, and many of those requests may contain mission statements that read more like essays than simple statements. You want your statement to stand out for being immediately clear.

Take some time now to write your mission statement. Make sure you can state your mission in one sentence, and ensure that it says precisely what it is you do. Show it to someone who is not involved in your organization. Is it clear to them? If not, what is unclear about it? If it is unclear, edit and pare it down, then show it to them again. When you have a clear mission, you are ready to move on to your next step.

# Chapter 2

## What is Your Vision?

O nce you have a clear and concise mission, you can expand upon it in your vision statement. The vision statement is your opportunity to put your long-term hopes and dreams for your organization into words. It should answer the question, "If this organization could become everything I hope for, what would it be in five years?" Your vision statement presents an image of what success will look like.

Your vision statement is the first place in your foundation grant proposal where you begin to state your goals in general terms — you will have the opportunity later in the process to set specific goals. This statement is essential in the grant writing process because it outlines your future goals, speaks of your values, and defines your future contributions to the community.

As you might guess, the vision statement will be a little more extensive than your mission statement. It can also be more challenging to put into words, as it asks you to dig a little deeper to explore your reason for this venture, and put that vision into words that others can understand. Remember, you are creating this statement and presentation not only for yourself, but also for people interested in your business. An organization's vision statement often has much to say to stakeholders, employees, and volunteers about how they should view the organization.

## Grant Seeking Tip

The most important question you might ask yourself as you create your vision statement is, "What do I value about this organization?"

At Amicitia Community Gardens, the vision statement reads: **"Amicitia Community Gardens is a friendly organization where all community members can come together to cultivate our connection to nature and each other by growing food locally. Amicitia Community Gardens envisions environmentally educated communities in which people of all ages and backgrounds are encouraged to learn how to garden, reconnect with the land, and connect with our community."**

Amicitia Community Gardens could not envision much more for itself. Their vision statement speaks to the environment, the community, and the food. It is a good vision — simple and concise.

The combined mission and vision statements for Amicitia Community Gardens provide the basic framework for the coming proposal. The proposal will further describe how Amicitia Community Gardens will put its mission into action and realize its vision. It will also propose how the funding foundation can work as a partner in this mission and vision.

Let us see what we have for Amicitia Community Gardens so far:

**Amicitia Community Gardens is a community gardening cooperative whose mission is to assist families, neighborhoods, and organizations**

**in growing food for themselves and the community. Amicitia Community Gardens is a friendly organization where all community members can come together to cultivate our connection to nature and each other by growing food locally. Amicitia Community Gardens envisions environmentally educated communities in which people of all ages and backgrounds are encouraged to learn how to garden, reconnect with the land, and connect with our community.**

As you can see, the mission and vision statement appear together in the above paragraph. This is how it will be presented in your proposal, but you may also use your mission and vision statements separately, depending on the guidelines of the foundation to whom you are submitting a proposal. Remember, the mission is the most important statement; the visions is an extension of the mission.

Consider what makes the mission and vision statements of Amicitia Community Gardens effective. First, the statements are easily read and understood; when you read or hear them, you know what they aim to achieve. Second, you essentially know how they plan on conducting their business. Also — and this is very important — the vision statement speaks to both the short-term and the long-term.

The vision statement speaks to the short-term by telling you that Amicitia Community Gardens is a friendly organization where community members come together to cultivate their connections by growing food locally.

The vision statement then takes a long-term look at the future by stating, "Amicitia Community Gardens envisions an environmentally educated community in which people of all ages and backgrounds are encouraged to learn how to garden, reconnect with the land, and connect with our community."

It is important to understand that the foundations you send proposals to have their own visions — they seek to give money to organizations and individuals that share their vision. If you delve into a foundation proposal without a vision for your organization and how it fits into the community-at-large, you have a lesser chance of receiving funding than those who enter the process with a clear vision. With a clear mission and vision statement, Amicitia Community Gardens now has a solid base from which to launch into the specifics of their funding proposal.

But it is important to further present the functions of the company seeking funding. These statements are what attract the funder to your proposal, but it is the rest of the proposal that will present how you will operate your business to abide by these statements.

## CASE STUDY: REBECCA JEWELL

Paul J. Strawhecker Inc.
4913 Dodge St.
Omaha, NE, 68132
**www.pjstraw.com**

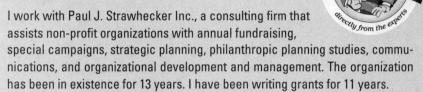

I work with Paul J. Strawhecker Inc., a consulting firm that assists non-profit organizations with annual fundraising, special campaigns, strategic planning, philanthropic planning studies, communications, and organizational development and management. The organization has been in existence for 13 years. I have been writing grants for 11 years.

Much of the funding I seek is for program, capital needs, or organizational capacity-building. I am most familiar with family foundations, community foundations, corporate foundations, and corporate giving programs. I have some experience with government funding, but that is not a special area of expertise for me.

The amount of money I receive as a result of foundation grant writing varies from year to year, but I would estimate it to be in the range of $500,000, give or take a hundred thousand or so. I do not tend to write the really big money grants to government sources or the large national foundation; I usually write to local or regional foundations.

The majority of grants I seek are associated with capital campaigns for building construction, renovation, or expansion. This includes historical renovation. Most of the clients of our firm are for capital campaign consulting. That said, I have certainly written my share of program grants, start-up grants, and capacity building grants.

What I think makes for a compelling grant proposal is:

1.  A succinct and logical connection between the funding and the results to be achieved

2.  A compelling impact statement on how the funding will make a difference to humanity

As a grant seeker, what I look for in a funder is a geographic connection to the organization I am writing for. This is usually my first qualification. Then, I look to see whether the funder has restrictions related to the type of funding I am seeking. Some prospective funders state that they do not give to capital, for example, or will not provide funding for staff salaries, or will only give to projects in the United States.

## CASE STUDY: REBECCA JEWELL

Among the foundations that I tend to write to — local, regional, family foundations — it is very common for foundation representatives to have personal connections to the agencies they fund, either through their own activities, as a user of the service, or through a family connection or an acquaintance with a board member or staff member. I think that most often, funders have connections to the agencies they fund. They do not award grants in a vacuum. Finding and building upon those personal connections is as important as writing a great proposal.

I advise any grant seeker to look at what organizations the funders give to in their official guidelines, publications, and/or Web sites, etc., but to also always look at what organizations they actually give to by viewing the IRS Form 990 whenever possible. Often, funders say they do one thing — and they probably strive to do that — but what they actually do can be something very different.

For example, I once sat in on a presentation of local family foundation representatives talking about how they award grants and their funding priorities. One man spoke about how the family does not like to take calls about potential proposals, but prefers to receive proposals or letters of inquiry to review. Then, he told about the largest award the foundation ever gave, which all started when an executive at the university saw him at a restaurant and shared his vision for a university program. The foundation rep was trying to explain that organizations need to share a great idea and that funders will respond to a compelling vision. What I took away from the presentation was that, even though they claim not to want personal calls or visits, the groups that get the really big awards are those that can make a personal call or visit.

I have had great success submitting "blind" proposals to another foundation in town, but I have seemed to hit the ceiling of award limit and can get only modest gifts from the foundation. It is very private. Even though you can reach them on the phone, they will tell you — politely but firmly — that they prefer not to have personal contact or calls regarding proposals. The organizations that receive the largest gifts have the foundation president on their board of directors. Obviously, there must be all kinds of personal contact there that impacts the size of gifts received.

It may be that a project appears to be outside the foundation guidelines. I do not recommend disregarding guidelines, but research may turn up a personal connection that proves fruitful. Or, you may see that the foundation does actually award grants in that area, and you may be able to turn up a personal link to the foundation that made that possible. Grant seeking is as much personal relationships and connections as it is writing a great proposal.

# Chapter 3

## The Importance of Organizational Strategy

If we were to look into the future of our community garden, what would we hope to see? Do you think that any organization is where the stakeholders of five years ago hoped it would be? Are you looking three to five years into the future of your organization? Or do you just look forward to getting through the current fiscal year? Should Amicitia Community Gardens look beyond the current growing season? As a young organization, you might exist month-to-month financially, but you still must have a view of the future if you are to realize your vision.

Having a vision for the future of your organization — and having a plan to ensure that your vision is realized — can make the future all that you envision it to be. While it is not absolutely necessary to have a long-term strategic plan before you write a foundation grant proposal, it will make any proposal you prepare much more competitive.

Before you begin to strategize for your future, you need to prepare by examining your present. You have already begun this process by creating your mission and vision statements. Everything you do on the road to creating a strategic plan will come out of these statements. Who are you? What is your role in the life of the community-at-large? What are your current resources? Once you know where you are, you can begin to envision where it is you want to go and what your goals are.

There is great value in the planning and setting of goals; planning for the long-term health of your organization sets the agenda for success. A long-term strategic plan acts as a road map not only for the current year, but also for three to five years into the future of your organization. When you can translate this long-term vision into a foundation grant proposal, the foundations can look at your organization as one that plans to be around for a while. Foundations do not want to give money to support organizations that cannot envision the next three to five years.

A good strategic plan also helps to set the stage for continuity. Long-term planning helps the transition from one year to the next, and from one board of directors to the next, making the organizational mission more about the organization than the individuals that guide the organization. Another benefit of long-term strategic planning — by the simple act of putting organizational mission, vision, and important goals into concise words — is that it helps the organization focus on its fundraising and volunteer development.

The plan of action can be accomplished over a period of about a month, developed in four strategic development committee meetings and several conferences with important organizational stakeholders.

A good place to start is to identify a committee of two or three individuals to take on the task. You should look for people for this committee who:

- Have historical knowledge of the organization and the community
- Have a vision for the future and the willingness to put words on paper

- Have a good grasp on what is important to the business
- Love talking to other people and are not afraid of asking tough questions
- Offer diversity to the group

The mission of this committee is to gather the thoughts and opinions of organizational stakeholders with the aim of constructing a strategic plan for the organization and meeting to discuss it. Assuming that the committee goes into its first meeting with a clear idea of the mission and vision of the organization, its first priority is a discussion of the organization's current situation. The questions asked during this initial meeting will vary from organization to organization. However, your questions should focus on the current strengths and weaknesses of the organization, as well as any current opportunities that exist. At this point in your discussions, nothing should be off-limits. This will present the opportunity for the committee members to brainstorm and develop some plans for creating the proposal.

Now that the mission is firm, the company's current situation has been assessed, and the organizational issues have been identified, it is time to have a second meeting. In this second meeting, you will outline your organization's strategic direction. You will set general goals, long-range goals, and objectives. In the end, the important thing is that you agree on how to address your organizational issues.

But we need to define the difference between goals and objectives. Goals are broad but clear statements that relate to an organization's overall intention. Goals break an organizational mission down into specific, achievable components and identify the results the organization wants to accomplish. Objectives, on the other hand, help to break down intricate organizational goals. Objectives are interim signposts that can be reached in shorter periods and in more clear-cut ways than goals. Objectives, therefore, should always be measurable.

Good objectives have five common characteristics that can be remembered using the acronym SMART:

- **S**pecific
- **M**easurable
- **A**chievable
- **R**ealistic
- **T**imely

An example of a general goal for our community garden might be lifted directly from the mission statement by saying that our goal is to assist families in growing food for themselves. An objective could then be to determine the number of families that the organization can assist over the period of a year. Another objective would be to identify and secure 25 plots of land where families that do not normally have access to land can plant gardens.

As you begin to think about fundable programs, objectives such as these are easily transferred from strategic plans to funding requests. When you can tie funding requests to organizational objectives that are bound closely to your mission, you build a solid case for funding.

A long-range goal for Amicitia Community Gardens might be "to grow food for the community." An objective would be to provide 50 pounds of fresh vegetables every week to a community food pantry. This, again, is a SMART objective that can easily translate into a request for funding.

Being able to communicate your general and long-range goals, as well as your objectives, to stakeholders is the best way to get the important feedback you need as you look to plan your activities. Knowing these goals and objectives is a crucial step toward building a strong foundation-grant proposal.

The period between meeting two and three of your strategic planning committee provides time for you to gather data as you prepare to plan specific activities in response to organizational issues. This is the time to be communicating with your stakeholders to get feedback. The more you communicate with your stakeholders, the better chance you have of them buying into your plans.

It is always good to recommend that, after each strategic meeting, the committee:

- Organizes what was discussed
- Puts the minutes of the meeting into an easy-to-read format
- Submits it to interested stakeholders for feedback

After you have determined your goals and objectives, it will be time to start planning activities. Activities state what you have to do to achieve your goals and objectives. Activities are, as the word implies, actions. An activity that Amicitia Community Gardens must engage in to provide 50 pounds of fresh vegetables every week to a community food pantry is to make contact or partner with a pantry.

At meeting three, you will, as a committee, discuss and debate the feedback you received regarding your goals. You likely received many opinions about what your activities might be according to the goals. Here is where your committee's experience comes into play as you decide the actions to be taken to achieve your goals. Some decisions you make will be based on historical facts relating to what works for your community and what does not; some decisions you make will be best guesses. Do not be afraid to try new things. The important result is that decisions are made and you strive to move forward. Your goals in this meeting should be to make decisions on active strategies to achieve your goals, both short- and long-term.

Now it is time to put it all on paper. Your plan should begin with your simple mission statement, followed by your vision statement. The balance of your plan should outline, point by point, the goals you have agreed upon for the coming year, followed by the activities to support those goals. Finally, state your long-term goals and the activities that will achieve them.

As you enter this planning process with foundation proposals in mind, it is important to include all aspects of the business in your plan. It is smart to include some type of budgeting information in your foundation proposal. You do not need to work out specific budgets for the next three to five years, but consider making budgetary goals part of your long-term plan.

The following example is Amicitia Community Gardens' simple, long-term strategic plan. Note the simplicity of form and the SMART objectives. Amicitia Community Gardens also has a more extensive plan on file that outlines specific budgetary initiatives, human resource development plans, marketing goals, and a number of other long-term strategic programs linked to its mission and organizational vision. The following plan has been constructed for use in resource development. This example will highlight a goal:

# Amicitia Community Gardens Long-Term Strategic Plan 2009

*Amicitia Community Gardens Community Garden (ACG) is a community gardening cooperative whose mission is to assist families, neighborhoods, and organizations in growing food for themselves and the community. Amicitia Community Gardens is a friendly organization where all community members can come together to cultivate our connection to nature and each other by* growing food locally. Amicitia Community Gardens educates and encourages people of all ages and backgrounds to learn how to garden, reconnect with the land, and connect with our community.

ACG carries out this mission through four programs: Family Garden Initiative, Neighborhood Garden Plots, Gardeners Mean Business, and Learning to Grow. Each of these programs is tied directly to the mission of ACG.

A professional staff manages ACG. The staff, at the time of this plan, is made up of four full-time and six part-time employees. The full-time staff consists of an executive director, an office manager, a gardens manager, and an education director. The part-time staff consists of three gardening associates, a farmer's market manager, an education associate, and a landscape associate.

The stakeholders are: our community of gardeners, volunteers, and students; ACG Board of Directors; ACG staff; ACG sponsors; ACG funders; collaborative businesses and agencies; and the community at-large.

This strategic plan will outline the goals, objectives, activities, resources, products, and outcomes of ACG as a whole in the organizational framework developed by the Board of Directors.

## Goal 1

*To assist families in growing food for themselves*

## Objectives

- *To increase the number of family memberships in ACG by 15 percent annually over the next three years*

- *To increase professional assistance available to families for the purpose of developing their own property or community garden plot by 15 percent annually over the next three years*

- *To increase seed stock available to families by 50 percent*

- *To improve communication among families involved in ACG programs for a more open exchange of ideas and information*

## Activities

- *Expand ACG community information program in neighborhood schools, neighborhood associations, churches, and other community-based institutions*

- *Partner with community colleges throughout the area to provide internships for students studying agriculture, horticulture, and landscaping*

- *Increase seed saving initiative by 50 percent to make greater seed stack available*

- *Expand the organizational Web site to include family forum area for use by neighborhood family gardeners*

## Goal 2

*To further the development of the Community Garden Initiative*

## Objectives

- *To have at least one community garden in each precinct of the city within the next three years*

- *To have a part-time Gardening Associate working at each of neighborhoods' community gardens within the next three years*

- *To begin seed stores associated with each community garden*

- *To increase advocacy efforts on behalf of community gardens*

## Activities

- *Begin three new community gardens in different city precincts per year for the next three years*

- *Increase funding available to hire and train nine part-time gardening associates over the next three years*

- *Recruit volunteers associated with each of the city's community gardens to begin seed saving and storage programs*

- *ACG staff will expand advocacy of community gardening by lobbying city to use space in three central city parks as "showcase" community gardens within the next three years*

## Goal 3

**To assist ACG member gardeners interested in the commercial options of gardening**

## Objectives

- *Make professional assistance available to gardeners interested in learning basic small business practices*

- *Make $100,000 in small business start-up grants available to community and family gardeners over the next three years*

- *Begin two new community co-op farmers' markets on the city's south and west side over the next two years*

- *Organize online seed sales initiative over the next year*

## Activities

- *Partner with community colleges to help make small business classes, such as basic bookkeeping and accounting, available to ACG members at a reduced rate*

- *Increase fundraising efforts to make $100,000 in grants available for small business development among member gardeners*

- *Procure space for community co-op farmers' markets on south-side within ten months and west-side over the next 24 months*

- *Develop Web site space for the online seed sales initiative*

## Goal 4

*Expand ACG educational initiatives*

## Objectives

- *Establish Gardener Green clubs in city public schools*

- *Establish community gardening classes in community colleges*

- *Offer community gardening workshops through city parks programs*

## Activities

- *Begin Green Garden clubs in 15 public schools each year for the next three years*

- *Begin Green Garden clubs in seven of the city's private schools each year for the next three years*

- *Develop curriculum for community gardening classes in community colleges over the year for class implementation within two years*

- *Develop curriculum for community gardening workshops to offer through city parks over the next year, with ten offerings available at six parks within the next two years*

Again, this is a brief example of what might be a more expansive strategic plan for the community garden. Each of the initiatives addressed at the beginning of the plan might have had any number of goals attached to them. Included with those goals would have been a number of objectives, and activities designated to achieve those objectives. Attached to this plan should be budget objectives and projections. We will also find human resource plans that could include volunteer objectives.

While the mission, vision, and goals of any organization are specific to that organization, the need to outline organizational goals, objectives, and activities is common amongst organizations. Even if you are reading this as an individual seeking foundation grants, it is essential that you understand the necessity of setting goals and objectives.

It is important to note, before we move on, that you can look at the short strategic plan outlined here and pull at least 16 fundable programs that make for solid grant proposals. We will revisit this plan several times as we work our way through writing an effective foundation proposal. We will employ the objectives and activities identified above to write several examples of foundation grants. Take a minute now to look at the plan and identify activities that you think would make for strong grant requests.

Also, note that most — if not all — of the objectives of the Amicitia Community Gardens' long-term strategic plan are specific, measurable, achievable, realistic, and timely. As we move forward into the specific activity of writing foundation grants, you will likely come to appreciate the importance of SMART objectives.

Long-term planning for the health, vitality, and growth of your organization can be one of the most satisfying activities that your Board can enter into. It puts you in touch with your organizational present and envisions a long, prosperous future.

# Chapter 4

## Organizational Assessment

It is well and good to have a concise mission, clear vision, and a plan of action, but you will need to show the foundations how you assess that plan and your activities in the end. Were you successful? How do you measure success? Having a plan in place to measure your organizational actions will show the funders that you are capable of assessing the program they support.

Assessing your actions, objectives, and goals at the end of a predetermined period of time or particular program, or at certain intervals during the year, is important. It allows you to determine your progress, change things that are not successful, or redirect resources to areas that need assistance.

It is a common pitfall to become occupied by the day-to-day struggles of running any business or organization. This can often lead an organization to lose sight of its goals and even its mission. Being able to reflect on your entire operation, or even a particular program, can give new life and energy to your activities. Assessment is a healthy — and often required — practice for your organization.

Assessing an organization and/or its programs is a data-gathering task. You are attempting to determine the successes or failures of your organization or of specific programs, and the data you gather will allow you to diagnose problems. What you are looking to define is a realistic picture of whatever it is you are assessing. Sometimes that picture is painful, as you may see a program that did not live up to your expectations; sometimes, you may be pleasantly surprised by a program's success.

Here are a few things to keep in mind as you develop your assessment:

1. Do not enter the process with preconceived answers. If you do this, you will often try to work the data to reflect your preconceptions.

2. Make sure that you get people involved in the assessment process. If you do this, you will ensure that your stakeholders will buy into the results and be committed to any changes that are required as a result of the assessment.

3. As you work through this process, remember to value everyone's opinion. You never know where a good idea might come from.

4. Finally, remember that this assessment is about the organization and not the individual. Do not point fingers at individuals to blame them for any organizational failures that may arise through this process.

If you are assessing a specific program, it is important that you know from the start what the goals of the program were. Let us go back to Amicitia

Community Gardens. An objective that we stated for this cooperative community garden was to identify and secure 25 plots of land where families that do not normally have access to land can plant gardens. Let us say that the organization received foundation funding to assist in this objective. There was a time period of a year in which they had to accomplish this; now, the year is up and it is time to assess the program objectives.

Any assessment process should be tailored to fit the needs of the organization. However, there are common assessment practices that we will want to follow.

Make sure that everyone is on the same page regarding the extent of the assessment. What are you assessing? Who is involved, and what are their responsibilities? How long do you expect the assessment to take?

Once you have the scope of the assessment nailed down, make sure that any important stakeholders are notified. If Amicitia Community Gardens is assessing the plot program they received funding for, they should let the funders know that the program assessment is under way. Is there any specific information the funder might require?

When everything is in place and all parties understand their roles, you can begin to collect data. The data you collect will be determined by the scope and nature of the assessment. Amicitia Community Gardens might look at how many plots of land it was able to secure. They would look at the number of families they were able to assist. They would get feedback from the families. Were they able to bring new stakeholders into their organization because of the program? What did and did not work with this program? What might be done better next time? Will there even be a next time?

During this process, you should take advantage of the opportunity to answer as many questions as possible. Seize this opportunity to learn about your programs and your organization.

After you have gathered as much information as you can, take some time to analyze the data. Summarize the data for stakeholders. Look at connections among various aspects of the program and your organization. How did the program affect your organization? Identify those who took part in the program, your stakeholders, and the primary issues related to this program and how they affect your organization,

After you have analyzed the data, review it with your organization and any important stakeholders. Make sure that before the information is released for public distribution, everybody in your organization has reviewed the results. Answer any questions that may arise.

Take stock of your organizational response. What do those closest to you think about your analysis? From the data you have gathered, from your analysis, and from the opinions of your stakeholders, you can now make recommendations regarding the plans of actions that come out of your analysis. Does anything about the program need to change? Use the information from analyzing the data and answering these questions to create active approaches for change in the future.

It is advantageous to be prepared. Many organizations have received foundation grants without doing any of this work; however, this kind of organizational preparation will show foundations that you are organized, serious about what it is you are engaged in, and worthy of their attention. Your foundation proposal, if you have done this work, is more likely to get serious consideration than the organizations that are not as well-prepared.

# Chapter 5

## Organizational History

An organization's history is an explicit view of why and how your organization came into existence. A well-written history of your organization is a good way to connect your mission and vision statements. You can find many organizational histories on the Internet. These statements are usually found under the "About Us" links on the organization's home page. Take some time to read some of these, especially those histories of organizations that are similar to yours; make note of their effectiveness. Determine what makes an organizations statement of history effective or ineffective, and pay attention to the various formats the histories are conveyed in. What works for some organizations may not work well for others.

## Grant $eeking Tip

When you write the history of your organization, you may consider having two versions of it. It could be worth your while to write a long, specific version of your history followed by an encapsulated version. The encapsulated version will probably be the one that you will include in most grant proposals.

The following is an example of an encapsulated organizational history of our example community garden:

*Amicitia Community Gardens is a community gardening cooperative whose mission is to assist families, neighborhoods, and organizations in growing food for themselves and their community. Amicitia Community Gardens is a friendly organization where all community members can come together to cultivate our connection to nature and each other by growing food locally. Amicitia Community Gardens educates and encourages people of all ages and backgrounds to learn how to garden, reconnect with the land, and connect with our community.*

*Amicitia, a Latin word that loosely translates to "friendship," was first established by a group of strong-minded and committed Westview neighborhood residents who, ten years ago, took part in a citywide program offered by the Nature Conservancy to create green spaces in urban neighborhoods around the country. The first Amicitia Community Garden was planted in a 70- by 70-foot vacant lot in the Westview neighborhood, a residential neighborhood that, at the time, appeared to be in poor condition. Much of the neighborhood is made up of large apartment buildings with very few single-family homes. The lot that Amicitia Community Gardens' first garden was planted on had been a vacant lot for nearly 20 years.*

*Because many of the residents of the Westview neighborhood are immigrant families, many of them have come from places where gardening and farming was an important way of life. Thus, the desire of the neighborhood residents to develop a community garden took root with a dynamic cause. The community was committed to stopping the appearance of poor conditions and establishing a little bit of 'home' in this new land.*

*That first Amicitia Community Garden was planted in the spring of 2001. At the time, 12 families took part in the garden's development. In that first year, the gardeners grew tomatoes, peppers, bok choy (an Asian vegetable in the cabbage family), carrots, cabbage, and several kinds of beans. Flowers were also grown around the garden's outside edge. Those who planted it enjoyed the garden's produce, and the entire neighborhood enjoyed the flowers. Sixteen families planted the garden the following year, and space was suddenly at a premium; more and more people were interested in Amicitia Community Gardens. Local television coverage of the garden in full summer ripeness made the entire city aware of our program in that second year. In April 2003, several of the gardeners were asked to visit classrooms in schools around the city to talk about neighborhood gardens. The children in several schools started plants inside their classrooms and, as the weather grew warmer, those plants were moved out into the schoolyards. Gardening activities were offered during the summer months with assistance by our neighborhood gardeners in order to maintain the school gardens throughout the summer and to further the children's knowledge of gardening.*

*The next two summers saw an explosion of the neighborhood gardening movement in the city, with Amicitia Community Gardens at the forefront of this wonderful growth. Six more urban lots in four different city neighborhoods became community gardens, and Amicitia Community Gardens' mission changed from that of a singular community garden to an organization whose mission is to provide places where all community members can come together to cultivate our connection to nature and each other by growing food locally.*

*As Amicitia Community Gardens grows and moves toward its tenth year, its commitment to community gardening and community growth blooms right along with it. Amicitia Community Gardens has begun establishing relationships with citywide food banks to provide fresh produce throughout the growing season, as well as fall/winter vegetables such as potatoes, sweet potatoes, and squash that will last into the winter. Relationships have been made with a number of upscale restaurants to provide fresh, locally grown herbs and vegetables during the summer months. Charitable and business opportunities abound for our neighborhood gardeners. A farmers' market has been established next to our first Westview neighborhood community garden to sell produce and flowers, and to spread the word about our program.*

*The future looks bright for Amicitia Community Gardens and community gardening. The first ten years have brought us a bountiful harvest, and we anticipate the abundance of the next ten seasons.*

Amicitia Community Gardens accomplishes a number of things with this short organizational history. They state their mission and describes how it came to be. They back the mission up with descriptions of how the mission and vision are supported. Several examples are given as to how important the organization has become to the community, and they make a good case for continued organizational growth. This is the kind of history that funders love seeing.

Amicitia Community Gardens could expand upon this history by giving a detailed description of the lots of garden it has acquired and when it acquired them. They could list partnerships made and when they were made. A number of different elements could be placed into a specific schedule of history detailing the organization's growth, but the example above serves as a good encapsulation of their history.

Amicitia Community Gardens, as you have read, is a healthy, 10-year-old organization. If you are reading this book, there is a good chance that you are contemplating raising funds for a younger organization or that you are an individual seeking funding. You might be wondering how to write the history of a 2- or 3-year-old organization. Just start from the beginning and keep it simple. Your history should include a short description of origin that supports your mission and vision.

Along with your organization's history statement, you should also have a financial record ready to show funders. Ideally, you should have a record of the past three years of independently audited financial statements, IRS filings, and budgets from the current year. We will get to the current budgets later, as we talk more directly about writing your proposal.

Whether you are a start-up organization, an organization in its third year, or heading into your tenth year like Amicitia Community Gardens, the importance of keeping your financial house in order cannot be overstated. One of the most important steps you can take is to do an independent audit every year. While it is important to keep up on your bookkeeping and keep your finances orderly, having an independent auditor put the unbiased stamp of accountability, transparency, and compliance to accepted accounting principles on your finances tells potential funders that you will also keep a close eye on the funds they grant you.

You may be required to show funders some of your past IRS filings. Most not-for-profits will have to produce several years of the IRS Form 990. Form 990 is the tax return filed by organizations exempt from federal income tax because they are designated as not-for-profit under section 501(c) 3 of the Internal Revenue Code.

If you are a not-for-profit organization or have a pending application for not-for-profit status, you have a federal ID number that designates you as such. If you have this status, you should have a history of 990s. In some cases, if you are a new or young organization, you can get by without including audited financial statements to your foundation grant proposal by only attaching your 990s. This does not imply that you should not have independent audits done; it just says that younger not-for-profit organizations might be able to get by for a year or two by including the 990 alone. If Amicitia Community Gardens, at ten years old, were to file a grant proposal and report that they had not been doing independent audits, the funders may wonder why.

Some foundations will only give grants to not-for-profit organizations. If this is the case, it is important to them that they only provide funding to organizations that are in compliance with the IRS. The foundations that give grants to organizations and individuals that are not recognized as not-for-profits will still expect financial accountability. Whatever the case, keeping your financial house in order will ensure that you can make a good case when your proposal is made.

One more piece of historical recordkeeping that we will cover here is the reporting of past grants. Not all foundations will ask for this information, but some will, and it is good to have an existing report of past funders. This record will detail any support you have received from foundations, corporations, businesses, government, and individuals. It is important to many funders to see that if they fund you, they are not alone, and that you and/or your organization have considerable support from the community at-large. If you have many people who have given you donations of $1, keep track of it. Sometimes, those small donations can be every bit as important as the large donations. As you make your case to foundations for that $25,000 grant, it is good to be able to say that you had 1,000 people make small donations to your cause, which shows strong community support. Also, be prepared to back this support up with your independently audited financial statements.

# Chapter 6

## Your Stakeholders

It is important at this point to expand on the notion of who you are. We have discussed your mission and organizational vision; we have explored your history and looked into you future via your long-term strategic plans; now it is time to identify what makes your organization work: the people. If you are an individual preparing to seek foundation funding, you have stakeholders, too. Your people are your stakeholders, and you likely have more than you think.

Whether you are a writer, an owner of a community garden, or a designer of energy-efficient housing, you affect the lives of people. People read your books, smell your flowers, and live in the neighborhoods where your houses are built. You touch many lives. The individuals who donate $1 to your cause and or write a check for $25,000 are all your stakeholders.

As you consider who your stakeholders are, you will conclude that some hold more stake than others — that is, they have donated more monetary funds to your organization. However, that $1 donor might be every bit as committed as the $25,000 donor. How much an individual or group gives every year is not necessarily a good way to judge commitment to your cause.

The ability to show potential funders that you are constantly working to expand your network of stakeholders plays well in your coming foundation proposal. Let us identify some of the stakeholders that funders will be interested in hearing about. Stakeholders are individuals, organizations, and businesses that support, work for, and/or are affected by you or your organization. Your stakeholders should comprise:

## Business Partners

You will describe your business partners and board members in your organizational plan. Foundations that you apply to are interested in seeing the structure of your organization. These stakeholders can provide outside associations that prove to be essential when looking for additional stakeholders.

## The Community You Serve

Your organization serves a specific community. The people within this community are your stakeholders. They are greatly affected by your organization and therefore depend on its funding. Foundations will be looking at the community you serve and how you serve them. When creating your organization plan, it is important to describe these stakeholders.

## Employees

As a part of your organizational plan, as in Amicitia Community Gardens' plan, you will describe the employee support you have. In the third paragraph of Amicitia Community Gardens' long-term plan we outlined earlier, we merely stated job titles, but you will want to have job descriptions on hand, as well. Your employees are vital organizational stakeholders.

## *Volunteers*

Volunteers are crucial stakeholders in many organizations. Your young organization may have a few volunteers, or maybe your organization is completely volunteer-driven. You may be like Amicitia Community Gardens and even have hundreds of volunteers. Your volunteers may provide office support, serve as board members, or come by once a year to help clean the parking lot. No matter what they do, volunteers are significant stakeholders to any organization. Do not forget them in your description.

## *Organization Members*

If you are a membership organization, your members are stakeholders. Every member of Amicitia Community Gardens is just as important as the person who writes the checks. Members are often both volunteers and check-writers.

## *Clientele*

If your organization sells tickets, goods, or services, then those who buy these items are stakeholders. It is important to have accurate records of your sales. It is strongly suggested that you know who your buyers are and how much they buy over the course of the year. Not only will your customers be presented to your foundation as stakeholders in your proposal, but your sales and profit information is needed for your budget and accounting records.

The stakeholders described above are defined as your clientele. Others may be those who are on your mailing list, visit your Web site, or perhaps consider your services because of a newspaper ad, article, or listing.

## *Foundations Who Support Your Organization with Grants*

The foundations, corporations, individuals, government entities, and associations that support your work with contributions are stakeholders, and it is important that you keep a good record of who they are and how they support you. If you write many grants, you will be asked about your stakeholders.

The important thing to remember about this group of stakeholders is that the better you know them, the better you know yourself — and the better you know yourself, the more effective your foundation proposal will be.

Your goal is to make sure that the foundation you are introducing yourself to, by way of a grant proposal, become a member of your inner circle of stakeholders. They do not want to be alone. Let them know that they will be in good company by showing them that you have a wide support network of people who share your vision and believe in your mission.

# Chapter 7

## What are Your Needs?

We are at the final chapter in this first section of our guide, and you are ready to start to build a case for funding as you seek to describe your organizational needs. What is mapped out here will go at the forefront of your request for funding. By now, you are set in your mission and have articulated it. Your vision is clear. You have a plan.

Now it is time to review the work you have done to determine and prioritize your needs. Like the preparation of your strategic plan, this task will take some time. Having your strategic plan completed is a big step forward in identifying your needs, however. You can look at Amicitia Community Gardens' strategic plan and identify numerous plans of action. The goal now is to determine what gets done first. Get people involved in the setting of priorities, as the input of stakeholders can help to make what may seem like a daunting task a little more manageable.

## Grant Seeking Tip

Always keep your mission in mind and at the forefront of any needs assessment. If you have done your strategic planning with this in mind, and you draft your foundation proposals straight from your strategic plan, this should not be much of a problem.

Consider the big-picture effect of a foundation proposal. What resources will it take to put the proposal together? What resources will it take to manage the proposal if it comes through? Getting a grant can be a wonderful thing — until you realize that you may not be ready to fully manage it the way it should be.

At this point, it is imperative to look at the objectives from your strategic plan and evaluate what your needs will be based on those objectives. Take this objective, for example:

- Partner with community colleges to help make small business classes (such as basic bookkeeping and accounting) available to ACG members at a reduced rate.

Also look at this activity:

- Develop curriculum for community gardening classes in community colleges over the year for class implementation within two years.

Both of these points are educational initiatives set out by Amicitia Community Gardens. These would require partnering with a college and developing a curriculum.

Amicitia Community Gardens probably does not require a foundation grant to partner with community colleges. They may require a foundation grant to develop a curriculum once the partnership is in place. Think of the temptation to apply as you research funding and begin seeing deadlines. You could be all ready to begin writing grants: You have all of your preparation finished. Your mission is solid, and the planning is complete. You get an e-mail from the XYZ Foundation that invites an application for a $25,000 grant that will fulfill a need you have, but a partner is needed. If you do not have a partner yet, do not submit your application; it is better to pass and wait until everything is in order.

Likewise, Amicitia Community Gardens should wait to seek funding for curriculum development until they have developed that partnership with the colleges. To do otherwise is a potential waste of time and resources that may result in having to return funding, thereby potentially damaging a healthy relationship with a funder.

Let us go back to Amicitia Community Gardens' strategic plan and consider several needs based on stated objectives and activities. We will focus on Goal 2: "To further the development of the Community Garden Initiative." This goal is at the heart of the organizational mission and is, historically speaking, the core reason for their existence. Listed at the top of the objective list for this goal is to have at least one community garden in each precinct of the city within the next three years. This is a wide-reaching objective that is directly tied to their mission. This objective is ripe for a foundation grant proposal.

The other objectives that are listed under Goal 2 are:

- To have a part-time gardening associate working at each of the neighborhood's community gardens within the next three years

- To begin seed stores associated with each community garden

- To increase advocacy efforts on behalf of community gardens

Amicitia Gardens undoubtedly considers each of these goals to be worthy enough to warrant a place in their long-term strategic plan, but as they prioritize their goals, they may feel that the initial objective is the most far-reaching and worthy of top priority when it comes to grant proposals. Decisions like this become more difficult the smaller your organization is. If you have a big development office with a development director, several associates, and grant writers, you are probably able to seek many grants simultaneously. However, if you are seeking funding for a small organization with limited resources and manpower, you must prioritize your search.

Consider Amicitia Community Gardens' decision to make at least one community garden in each precinct of the city within the next three years a priority. Once that happens, they will be able to make a better case for having a part-time gardening associate at each of the community gardens. They will have a greater ability to begin seed stores associated with the gardens, and they will have a greater need and louder voice as they increase advocacy on behalf of community gardens.

Let us return to the challenges of small not-for-profits. Most small organizations have many needs, and prioritizing them can be overwhelming. If you ask these organizations what their greatest need is, they might reply, "money." Not-for-profits are notoriously under-staffed and almost always short of funds. If you work for such an organization, you may believe that you need to apply for every grant you hear about in order to get all the grant money you can. But never seek grant money just for the sake of it. This is called "grant chasing," and it is a strategy that will hurt you in the long-run.

Grant chasing is a dangerous game to play. It sets your organization as a company that does not have a decent program to pitch on its own, so it is forced to chase down every grant it hears about, trying to squeeze its program into the criteria to obtain any type of funding at all.

Another danger of grant chasing is making your organization and its programs constantly fit a foundation's criteria instead of meeting the needs of your community, which can lead your project in the wrong direction and far away from your initial mission.

A better course of action is to determine the scope of your project: what it is, who it will serve, and what it will cost. Then investigate foundations that have an interest in funding the exact type of program or service that your community needs — and that your organization is trained to supply.

Every not-for-profit organization needs money on a regular basis for operations, programs, salaries, and other needs. Keep in mind that grants should not be counted on as a means to keep your doors open and pay the bills on a regular basis. Sure, there are grants that may help you in this regard, but you will have more success as a grant seeker by seeking grants for programs, staff development, technology, or anything that more directly supports your mission. There is a list in the next chapter that will help you translate your needs into the language of the philanthropic community. Once you understand the basic rule of grant acquisition and the language necessary to translate your needs into the funder's objectives, it will be much easier to get the money you need to start and maintain the projects that your organization feels most passionate about.

## Grant Seeking Tip

To be successful at obtaining grants, you must first learn how to identify your needs and determine which of those needs is grant-worthy. You need to decide what projects and programs your organization needs outside funding for, and which ones can be successfully funded through traditional fundraising activities and events. If you can easily raise $1,000 to buy new study guides with a dinner or bake sale, raise it that way; it will likely be faster and easier than applying for a $1,000 grant.

If you discover that you have run out of options after tapping every re-source, and you determine that you still need money to meet a par-ticular goal, then consider exploring foundation grant opportunities to help fund the project. Remember, the awarding process can take six to 18 months.

Here are a few questions concerning your needs that may help you in de-termining whether your program or project is grant-worthy:

- Is this a fairly long-term project? In other words, can you wait the necessary time to get through the arduous grant process and receive your grant monies, or are you in immediate need of the funds? Some foundations may help you expedite the process in an emer-gency situation, and some foundations have grants that are specifi-cally designated as quick-fix funds. However, never rely on grants as a quick fix.

- Can we get money for this project any other way? Foundations do not usually want to fully fund projects or programs unless they have worked with your organization previously. They frequently look to provide 10 to 30 percent of the total cost, which requires your organization to find the balance of the funds elsewhere. The more money you have been able to raise for the project, and the more support you can gather before applying for a grant, the better chance you have of being awarded the grant money. Foundations want to know that others in your community are supporting your program before they are willing to risk their own funds on it.

- Do we have a clear sense of this project? Do we understand what will be involved in implementing it? Who will benefit from it? Are we certain as to the overall cost of the program? To be truly grant-worthy, a project or program must be well-developed with a strong and comprehensive outline of every phase of its activities, including a final plan for assessment.

- Does our project meet the foundation's current giving interest and size? We will get into the specifics of this question in later chapters, but it is good to mention it here. Never approach a foundation that has never given to a similar organization or project as the one you are proposing unless you have a reason to believe that they are expanding their guidelines and criteria. Also, look to see how much their average giving is before asking for a set amount of money. If most of the grants they award are between $10,000 and $25,000, do not ask for $250,000.

After you have determined your needs and that your project or program is grant-worthy, start looking at the foundations that may be interested in hearing more about what your organization can offer your community — with the right funding, of course. It is better to approach the foundation as a partner than to go in with your hand out. As you consider needs, a good thing to keep in mind is that you are always in need of a good partner.

## CASE STUDY: FELIX A. ROY - PROFESSIONAL GRANT WRITER

Felix A. Roy, M.S.
Grant Writer
13 Clamer Avenue
Collegeville, PA 19426
866-663-6244 – voice/fax

Researching foundations can be time-consuming. With thousands of different foundations out there giving away money for thousands of different types of projects, it is especially important to match your organization with just the right giver in order to be successful.

When researching foundations, I have discovered one of the most important elements to success is truly understanding the funding stream areas of giving and searching for foundations whose giving patterns best represent the organization's needs.

It is a fundamental reality of the tax law that foundations have an ethical and legal responsibility to give away a certain amount of money each year. It is your organization's need for this money for specific, worthy causes that gives it 501(c)(3) tax-exempt status by the IRS. Your job as a grant writer is to help match the foundation and their responsibility to give their money away to your organization's need and (IRS-recognized) worthiness. By doing so, you are actually serving both of them in helping each meet their own individual responsibilities.

In addition, know the foundation's rules before applying. No matter how worthy your cause, a great amount of time and energy can be wasted if you are simply applying to the wrong place.

# Chapter 8

## Common Grant Categories

Now that you are at the point in this process where you are considering your needs and beginning to explore the funding sources available to assist you in fulfilling those needs, you can start to link your needs to the greater funding community. Here is where you will begin to match your needs to the needs that foundations are looking to support. It is fitting that this chapter will bring us to the close of this first part of your quest, Know Yourself, and leads us into Section 2: Know the Funding Community.

It is easier to ask for money — and get it — when you understand the types of grants that an individual foundation may award. Here is a list of some of the most common grant categories being funded today:

- **Start-up or Seed Funding**: New organizations, or those wishing to initiate a brand-new program, may request start-up or seed funding in order to get their project up and running. This type of grant often helps to pay all sorts of initial set-up costs, including the first one to three years' salaries, rent, utilities, program materials, and other expenses. Seed funding is regularly reserved for the first one to three years of expenses in order to "get the ball rolling," and is not intended to cover your costs on a long-term basis; permanent funding must be sought elsewhere.

- **Capacity Building**: Much the same as start-up grants, but these are aimed at organizations that are past the start-up phase and are looking to grow in some respect. Capacity building grants might be used for marketing, public relations, fund development, or any area that an organization might need to grow organizational capacity.

- **Basic Operations**: Probably the most sought-after type of funding, grants for basic operations can be used to pay salaries, rent, marketing expenses, or just about anything an organization requires in its day-to-day business.

- **Professional Development**: Grants for professional development may be used for seminar, conference, or other types of training fees to help better equip your staff for running your organization. It may also include the hiring of a specific title, such as the starter salary for a fundraising consultant or a director of development. Most organizations understand the importance of hiring these types of individuals but simply lack the initial funds to make the hiring commitment, so they turn to a foundation grant to add the position to their payroll for the first year or two.

- **Capital / Capital Improvement Grants**: These grants are often used to pay for a new building project or expansion or to help cover the cost of needed renovations and emergency-type building issues (e.g., a new roof or a better heating system).

- **Technology Grants**: Most not-for-profit organizations lack the money necessary to keep their programs running using the best, most modern technology available. To help keep their computers, phone systems, and other technology areas up-to-date, many foundations are eager to fund specific technological upgrades and programs.

- **Program Costs**: For some organizations, finding the money to sustain a program can be difficult. There is always a need for new supplies and materials, advertising, staffing, and other expenses to be considered. Program grants are meant to help fill in the gaps between the money generated for big-ticket items associated with running the program and its daily expenses.

- **Scholarships**: Some organizations charge fees for their programs to members, students, or other clients and/or stakeholders. However, there are always those who cannot afford the service, so foundations may consider grants to cover the tuition or fees of those who need the service but are unable to pay for it.

Take some time now to look back at Amicitia Community Gardens' strategic plan, particularly the objectives and activities they have identified. Translate those objectives and activities into the grant areas identified in the list of grant types above. Example: An activity identified under Goal 1, to assist families in growing food for themselves, is the expansion of the organizational Web site to include a family forum area for use by neighborhood family gardeners. If Amicitia Community Gardens were to seek foundation funding for this activity, they might seek a technology grant to improve their Web site and accomplish this activity.

See whether you can go through this list of eight different grant types and identify an objective or activity that Amicitia Community Gardens could match up to each. In some cases, programs and activities might qualify in several different areas.

## CASE STUDY: MICHAEL FRANCO

The Open Fist Theater Company
6209 Santa Monica Blvd.
Los Angeles, CA 90038
**www.openfist.org**

The Open Fist Theater Company is an arts organization that has been producing theater in Los Angeles for 17 years. I have been writing grants for ten years.

Most of the grants I have written, and grant awards I have received, pertain to travel and matching funds for new and world premiere productions of new work. I have also written and received grants for the productions of my own work.

The amount of money we receive as a result of our grant-writing activities varies greatly; it all depends on the projects we engage in every year. It is a project-by-project scenario. We look for money for running the organization, funding new work, helping with our rent, about anything… mostly to help with our rent and facilities, and travel for taking our work abroad.

I think that what makes for an intriguing grant is excitement. There has to be excitement in the project or organization. I think the excitement of your project needs to be contagious.

When I look for funders, I am looking for organizations that are interested in promoting new work and helping the producer bring that work to life. What I think funders find attractive about our organization is that we produce new work that is groundbreaking and exciting.

Advice I would give to new grant writers is to write your grants with a single voice, so that the reviewing funder can read about the excitement and passion you have for your project.

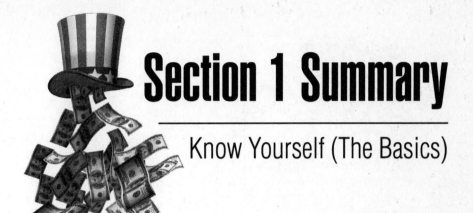

# Section 1 Summary

## Know Yourself (The Basics)

If you have followed along with the book and written each part of your proposal as we went through the process, you now have most of what you need for a solid foundation proposal. If a foundation called you tomorrow and asked you to submit a proposal, you would be ready. You are ready to answer just about any question they might ask you about your organization, and you have at your fingertips the information and data you need to inform them about your programs and activities.

You have a mission. Your vision is clear, and you can see your organization's past, present, and future. You have done your research and have your financial house in order. You have independently audited financial statements and your IRS Form 990s. You have learned about writing a proposal; now, it is time to learn about the funders.

# Section 2

## Knowing the Funding Community

If you have followed along with the book and written each part of your proposal as we went through the process, you now have most of what you need for a solid foundation proposal. If a foundation called you tomorrow and asked you to submit a proposal, you would be ready. You are ready to answer just about any question they might ask you about your organization, and you have at your fingertips the details and data you need to inform them about your programs and activities.

You have a mission. Your vision is clear, and you can see your organization's past, present, and future; you have done your research and have your financial house in order. You have independently audited financial statements and your IRS Form 990s. You have learned about writing a proposal; now, it is time to learn about the funders.

# Chapter 9

## Who are the Philanthropists?

As you think about funding options for your project, program, and/or organization, you have many things to consider. You should, by now, have a good handle on your needs. Now is the time to consider who can best fill those needs. If you are a young organization that is new to the world of fundraising, the best advice is to develop a well-rounded fundraising program. This book is about seeking foundation support, true, but it is worth your while to look into support from other avenues, as well.

If you have a well-rounded fund development program, you need not sweat as much when one aspect of it suffers. Consider that if you rely solely on government funding, and the government decides to slash funding to the arts, renewable resources, or community gardens, you may suffer some loss. You may, in such cases, have to make the difficult decision to cut staff, cut programming, or, in a worst-case scenario, close up shop. However, if appropriate grant opportunities are being sought after, hopefully you can avoid these situations.

Here is a quick rundown of a few of the main types of funding agencies that you may want to consider contacting for grant opportunities:

## Family Foundations

Family foundations tend to be quite small and give to extremely specific and individual causes. Though these foundations are small, this does not mean that they have small assets. Most family foundations started with the sole purpose of funding a specific type of program that may have affected the family in the past. For instance, if a child in the family has died of a certain disease, the foundation may fund medical research or expenses associated with that particular disease. Carefully study the foundation's guidelines and given interests before submitting your funding request to save yourself time and energy. Be aware that few small family foundations accept unsolicited proposals or requests due to their inability to either review or fund many projects on an annual basis. It is not unusual to discover these small foundations through word-of-mouth.

## Private Foundations

Private foundations often begin as small family foundations, but when they become too large for the family to run themselves, the foundation hires a small staff and trustees to handle the day-to-day operations and funding disbursements. This does not mean the family is no longer involved in the decision-making process; many family members may be on the board of directors, which makes all final disbursement decisions and grant awards. It does mean, though, that the foundation has become too large to be handled independently and, therefore, may offer organizations a few more funding opportunities than before, when it remained a family foundation.

# Public Foundations / Community Foundations

Commonly foundations, funds, and trusts are established by a group of individuals who would like to offer grant opportunities to their community, but are unable to establish a foundation on their own. These funds are then pooled together with the intention of providing funds to the local area. As with all foundations, the scope of giving interest for a community foundation might be exceptionally limited — only offering grant money for exceedingly specific purposes and needs — or it can be exceptionally broad. It all depends on the foundation's original mission and purpose. While individual donors may suggest certain grant recipients, it is ultimately up to the foundation's board of directors or trustees to make the final decision regarding all grant requests.

# Federated Funds

Federated funds allow businesses, corporations, and individuals to pool funds to benefit the community at large. The United Way is a good example of how federated funds work. Unlike a public or community foundation, which pools funds from individuals who are unable to start their own foundations, federated funds are established solely with the purpose of creating a large-scale funding option for the community and often rely on continual fundraising efforts to keep funds available.

# Government Agencies

Local, county, state, and national governments often allocate a certain percentage of monies to go toward community development in order to help individual communities better meet their needs — whatever those needs may be. Government grants are often available to schools, hospitals, fire and police departments, public sports organizations, historic preservation, and open-space initiatives, among others. These grants are almost always awarded to secular organizations whose main goal is to improve the community or its infrastructure in some way.

## Corporations

Corporate foundations are company-sponsored foundations that work as independent foundations created by the corporation and funded solely by it and its employees. Corporate foundations frequently award grant money within their interest area only. For instance, pharmaceutical corporations will, more often than not, only award grants within the health care or medical research industry, while a publishing house may award grants for literacy and education.

Another area of support that would be entered as unearned income on your budget is the area of individual contributions. This form of support is not a grant, but rather a straight contribution. This contribution can come in the form of cash, a donated used car, stock, from an insurance policy, or many other ways.

If you are raising funds for a not-for-profit organization, it is important to have a broad base of support. Get to know and understand the entities listed above. Establish relationships not only with foundations, but with local businesses, corporations, government entities, and individuals. As we discussed earlier in this book, it is vital to the life of your organization that you always seek opportunities to network.

# Chapter 10

## Philanthropy

The mission of this chapter is to learn about the foundations you will be writing your funding proposals to, why they give, and what they are giving. In the same way that defining your mission and vision helped you define who you are and what your business is, you will have to understand the motivations of the philanthropic community you seek to form partnerships with.

Fundraising in this manner — that is, searching for and writing foundation grants — is not an overnight act. It takes time to develop contacts, make your inquiries, write your grants, and wait for the foundations to make decisions. You do not want to go through this long process to discover that the foundation to which you have applied is not able to grant your request due to their declining assets. Research why Foundation XYZ awards grants, make sure your information is up-to-date, and ensure that the foundation is able to give.

It is important at this point to examine the difference between seeking grants and fundraising. Seeking grants is fundraising, but fundraising is more than just seeking grants. In both cases, though, you are involved in the world of philanthropic giving. Sometimes the line between seeking grants and fundraising can be hazy, especially when the responsibility for obtaining all types of funding for an organization falls to one person or a single group of people. It is common for some organizations to hire a "fundraising" or "development" officer whose main responsibility is to generate enough private funding, or unearned income, to maintain the organization's programs and plan for future projects. Other types of unearned income are grants, government funding, and any other funding that is realized through donations. Having a fundraising officer seek funding from all of these avenues will be beneficial to the organization.

This officer might be required to fill many roles in order to raise the money needed. If you find yourself in this situation, the important thing to remember is that grant writing and stewardship are only a part of the overall task of fundraising.

Fundraising requires:

- Planning events
- Establishing and maintaining good contact with individual donors
- Brainstorming new and better ways to raise income from the community
- Budgeting long-term

Pursuing grants, on the other hand, requires:

- Researching individual foundations and government agencies
- Understanding whom and what they prefer to fund
- Establishing a project that meets a funders criteria
- Getting funders interested in the organization and programs

Monies generated from fundraising activities such as individual donations and fundraising events can often be used for any purpose within your organization, such as supplies, salaries, program costs, and even utilities. Grant monies, however, are usually awarded for a specific purpose and must be used solely for that purpose. A detailed proposal and budget must accompany each grant request and be followed for every expense, with no deviation unless pre-approved by the funding agency. When that project or program has been completed, you will report back to the foundation with a project assessment to let them know what effect their funding had on the project and the organization.

One of the biggest tasks of the individual charged with researching and writing foundation grants is exploring who is likely to give to the organization and why.

The "whys" are often determined by philanthropic trends. Like your business, philanthropy does not occur in a vacuum. The economy, politics, social movements, and any one of a number of influences affect what happens in the world of foundations. A foundation that has supported the arts for years may decide that controlling the AIDS epidemic will demand all of their resources. A foundation that put a great deal of resources into protecting the endangered gray wolf may have decided that the wolf is no longer threatened as much as it once was, and might now funnel their resources into clean water.

The point is that it is up to you to be aware of these trends before you spend your valuable time seeking assistance. It is your responsibility to understand why the foundations you approach support such causes.

A strong economy has a positive impact on giving, and a weak economy slows or halts giving altogether. Smaller foundations may be more affected by a weak economy than larger foundations, and corporate foundations may be affected by economic downturns in different ways than private foundations.

When the economy takes a downturn, foundations adapt to this change in several different ways:

- They may alter the size or number of grants
  - *Offering fewer grants with higher payouts*

- They may change the scope and/or focus of their grant initiative
  - *Offering priority to certain projects*

- They may cut their own administrative costs
  - *Trimming staff*
  - *Creating a more efficient administrative structure*

As the mission of the foundation is to provide resources for grant making, many foundations opt to cut administrative costs before they cut grant opportunities, thus it is important to stay up-to-date on economic trends as they affect philanthropy. A good place to keep an eye on trends in philanthropy is *The Chronicle of Philanthropy*®, The Newspaper of the Nonprofit World (**http://philanthropy.com/**). With this excellent resource, you can keep abreast of trends in giving.

While researching the financial situation of the foundation you are seeking funding from, research the guidelines of the grant as well. Sometimes the guidelines are quite clear in their descriptions of what they support. Example: "The Bill and Melinda Gates Foundation$^{SM}$ is dedicated to bringing innovations in health and learning to the global community." This mission of the Bill and Melinda Gates Foundation$^{SM}$ is a pretty simple and direct statement — as it should be. There are more exact specifications on its Web site, but this statement should be sufficient to let you know if it is a foundation you should seek funding from.

Foundations often look for more than organizations whose vision they share; they look for organizations that they believe are in business for the long-term. Most foundations do not want to make a donation to an organization that will not be around next year. The long-term strategic plan and organizational finances will be a good indicator of an organization's plan for the future. As you begin to read the foundation guidelines, make sure that you are able to comply with the information they request from you.

Many foundations give to organizations they want to be involved with. Foundations may give priority to organizations in communities where the foundation is also active because they want to work to make the community a better place to live and/or do business. The word "community" in this context means the community in which the foundation is physically located and does business. It might refer to the health care community, the arts community, or the ecology community.

Some foundations give to become more involved in an organization, and might request a seat on the board of directors. They might have employees work as active volunteers or provide services to the organization.

Understanding the "whys" of each foundation you consider approaching for funding will greatly increase your ability to write a proposal that will be heard. It is your responsibility to do your research and remain up-to-date on philanthropic trends, foundation guidelines, and events that affect your world — and theirs.

## Grant Seeking Tip

As you explore potential foundations, keep a checklist of basic questions to consider about each one. The questions on your list might include:

- What is the foundation's vision?
- Do we share visions?
- Does the foundation support organizations in this community?
- If the foundation turns us down for funding, can we go back to them in the future?

Your list will expand and change over time, but you will find that keeping such a checklist will make weeding through the many foundations a little easier.

Part of getting to know a foundation is understanding what it has to give. — that is, knowing what exactly a grant is. Maybe it is best to start by saying what a grant is not.

A grant is not:

- A gift
- A donation

Gifts and donations are usually given unconditionally. A grant is awarded based on a proposal, and the foundation expects the proposal they are funding to be successfully carried out. Therefore, it is not a gift or a donation.

It is rare for a foundation to hand over checks equaling thousands of dollars with no clear understanding of what the money it is offering will be used for. Unlike a monetary donation, which may be used by an organization for any purpose, a grant is a monetary award given to an organization or individual to carry out a specific activity. The funder — whether it is a foundation, corporation, or government agency — expects the grant award to be used to help the recipient carry out the project or program detailed in the proposal submitted.

Grants are most often awarded on a basis of community need and the organization's ability to provide services not available elsewhere. For instance, an individual — or even a company — might decide to donate funds to your organization to be used for a building project, ongoing support costs, or any other project you might need money for. While they can tell you what project or program the money must be used for, they cannot tell you exactly how the funds should be used within the program itself.

Therefore, if Amicitia Community Gardens wanted to use a donation earmarked to their Community Garden Initiative to hire more associate gardeners, they would be free to do so. If, however, they were awarded a grant from a foundation to purchase seeds for the Community Garden Initiative, they would be required to use the money for that purpose only, regardless of what other needs might arise. Of course, they are free to request a funding change with the foundation awarding the grant, but that often requires the submission of an entirely new application and proposal; this could result in the grant funds being retracted. Changes become easier the more you get to know the funder.

The important lesson to take away from this chapter on the "who" and "why" of philanthropy can also be gleaned from nearly all the case studies in this book. Get to know the funder. As you enter a relationship with a foundation, remember that you are entering into a partnership that is defined by the value of your activities as partners. You are going into this partnership to help make your community a better place. The XYZ Foundation is able to make sure that the urban neighborhoods of their city are green because of the work of Amicitia Community Gardens. The XYZ Foundation provides grants to Amicitia Community Gardens so that the community garden organization, in partnership with the foundation, can assist families with planting and harvesting gardens.

## CASE STUDY: DR. JACQUELINE E. BROWN, EXECUTIVE DIRECTOR

Atlanta Children's Shelter
607 Peachtree Street
Atlanta, GA 30308
**www.acsatl.org**

The Atlanta Children's Shelter (ACS), in existence since July 1986, provides loving, quality child development and support services for homeless families striving to become self-sufficient.

ACS has been seeking and writing foundation grants since its inception in 1986. In addition to foundation grants, ACS searches several funding streams: individuals, employee groups, service organizations, corporations, religious groups, United Way, and limited government grants. In 2008, we received $223,890 from foundations, compared to a budgeted goal of $130,000.

A compelling grant proposal is made by a case for support that is well-articulated with a good "story" to tell, solid statistical data, a strong organizational track record, financial stability, alignment of request with current needs, and strategic planning goals.

While there are many potential funding sources we could pursue, we try to evaluate the potential offered by each segment under consideration. (We do not "chase" dollars). Consideration is given to the quality as well as quantity of donors to pursue. For grants, we look for clear guidelines in the RFP (Request For Proposals) to ensure that we have resonance with the prospective donor and that there is a proper match. What are the funder's criteria for grant submission? How complex/complicated is the application process? What are their evaluation procedures?

In 2005 and 2008, ACS was selected by the Community Foundation for Greater Atlanta as a finalist for their annual Managing for Excellence Award. The Selection Committee cited the following reasons for their decision: sound fiscal management and diverse sources of annual support, including 21 percent from individuals; the leadership was another contributing factor, citing the respectful and collaborative management environment created by the long-term executive director. Board involvement is crucial to a well-managed organization, and the committee felt that the ACS Board Chair clearly linked the shelter's mission, programs, and future direction. ACS has been recognized as a national best-practices model agency.

## CASE STUDY: DR. JACQUELINE E. BROWN, EXECUTIVE DIRECTOR

If managed well, foundation fundraising can be creative, deliver high returns, and produce lasting, profitable relationships with key funders. All foundations are different; however, there appears to be some consistent patterns in their grant-making preferences. I have heard from foundation representatives that the single biggest mistake seen by donors is inaccurate proposals. Also, the agency  does not follow the RFP guidelines or rules. Do not use "boiler plate" language, especially if the donor only funds programs — not operating. Sustaining donors deserve the opportunity to hear what/how you are doing on an ongoing basis. Have a well-rounded communication mechanism in place year-round of the organization's progress/successes/challenges. When prospecting new sources, know who the "gatekeeper" is in order to get to a person (e.g., know the secretary's name).

Donors are not ATMs. They are driven by needs and wants, and they give based on an exchange of values: to do the right thing; to create a return on investment; to enhance self-worth. I have found that donors are loyal to charities that are perceived to be leaders; provide relevance and meaning; and offer significance and fulfillment.

# Chapter 11

## How Funding Decisions are Made

L et us go back to the beginning of the relationship between Amicitia Community Gardens and the XYZ Foundation — back to the time when the foundation had never even heard of Amicitia Community Gardens. Amicitia Community Gardens, our fictional community garden, was a 10-year-old organization with a wonderful mission and a clear vision. They had gotten a little press, and things were just starting to take off for them. The founding director of the organization was doing all the developmental work, such as finding, researching, and writing all the grants; putting all the budgets together; and writing all the thank-you letters to everyone who provided funding — even the $1 supporters. Let us call the founding director "Rose." You may be the Rose in your organization.

Rose did all her preparation to research and write an effective grant. She made sure the mission and vision statements were clear. She worked with her board of directors on the organization's long-term strategic plan. She wrote the organizational history you read earlier in this book. She identified the XYZ Foundation as a foundation that makes grants of up to $10,000 to not-for-profit organizations that promote connections among people, plants, and the environment. Perfect. This was to be Rose's first attempt at grant writing. She put all the pieces together and got her grant in on time. "Now what?" she wondered. "What happens to the grant once it is delivered to the XYZ Foundation? How will the decision be made?"

Rose learned all her lessons well. She learned the importance of getting to know her potential funders. Then she got to know the foundations in-depth before she applied for her grant. She even thought about how the funders would look at her and what lengths they would go to check out Amicitia Community Gardens' credibility. So, she had all the answers she needed. This does not mean that all foundations go through the same process in determining exactly whom to fund and how much they are going to give. There are probably as many processes as there are foundations. However, we will take time here to review what exactly the funders will look at when they consider your (or Rose's) proposal.

No foundation is likely to hand over thousands of dollars to an organization merely on a promise. They expect their grant recipients to know how to handle the programs they are proposing and will require them to prove it before disbursing any funds. Think about that when putting together your proposal and it will be easier to present yourself and your project in a successful way.

Here are a few things foundations look at when considering applications:

- **Not-for-profit status**: Many foundations will not even begin to consider giving grants to individuals or organizations that are not recognized not-for-profit corporations. Before applying for funding, make sure you know what the foundation's policy is in this regard.

- **Mission and vision**: Most foundation reviewers will look deeply into your organizational mission and vision when considering funding. Many foundations will also look into your organization's and board's affiliations as they regard your proposal. Foundations rarely support organizations and projects that go against their own belief systems. Be sure that yours match, or be prepared to prove why your project is important enough to overlook any discrepancies between your views and the foundation's.

- **The rationale for applying for a grant in the first place**: Think about whether it makes sense to apply for a grant to fund your project. Consider other sources of income and let the foundation know why you have chosen to take this route for funding. Also, consider the reasons why you chose a particular foundation. You know that they have given money to similar projects in the past. Do not be afraid to mention other recipients in your proposal. For instance, if the foundation you contact regularly awards grants to a local homeless shelter, and you are offering an extension service geared toward the same demographic group, mention in your cover letter or proposal how you intend to help the people living at the shelter obtain important jobs skills. Most foundations have a heart for a specific group of people and their needs. If you find a way to tap your project into those needs, your chances of getting a grant rise sharply.

- **If there is a true need**: Having a program that meets a need is also important when applying for a grant. The key to obtaining grant money is proving that you need the foundation's help to make your program a success. While you must be able to sustain the project with other resources once the grant money has all been used, you must still show the necessity of obtaining the foundation's funds in order to complete the work ahead.

- **What the foundation has to gain**: Many foundations, and especially corporations, give money to specific organizations for the publicity it generates. Offer to name a room or a part of a project after their foundation; establish a publicity plan that will give them free press; or share ways in which you will publicly thank them for their generosity (e.g., a banquet or a plaque). Also, tie-in ways for the foundation to publicize their grant award in-house. Mention your organization's willingness to be featured in their annual report, to speak at a press conference or banquet regarding the good works of the foundation, or suggest other ways that will help them develop within the industry and community.

- **The organization's credibility**: A potential funder will look at your organizations credibility. Make sure to include as much good press as possible in your proposal. This might include:

  - Recent articles printed in the local media highlighting your programs and services
  - A complete list of all board members and their affiliations
  - Any awards your organization, staff, or board members have received
  - A rundown of other projects you have successfully completed
  - A listing of all other foundation grants you have received

If your organization has had to face any unpleasant issues that garner publicity, do not try to hide it; the foundation will find out anyway. Be honest, and explain how your boards of directors and staff have worked to overcome any negative outcome to whatever struggles you have faced, and how you have learned from the experience.

- **The organization's ability to implement the project being proposed**: Some of the things that a funding prospect will look into are financial stability and the support available to continue your efforts for the long-term. They look to see if you have sufficient space and materials, an adequately sized and trained staff, and a need for this particular project. Be prepared to answer these questions and concerns yourself so that the foundation will not have to find the answers elsewhere.

- **The appearance of your application:** A professional, well-thought out application can have a direct bearing on whether you get the grant you seek. Grant applications that look like they were put together quickly and effortlessly are rarely taken seriously.

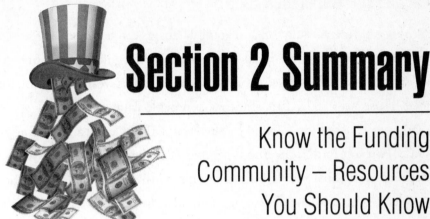

# Section 2 Summary

## Know the Funding Community — Resources You Should Know

You can never know everything there is to know about the foundations you submit proposals to. You can prepare yourself, however, by thoroughly educating yourself. If you follow the guidelines presented in this book, you will be better prepared for the process that takes place after you submit your proposal. You are not going to get every grant that you apply for. Sometimes, the decisions that are made may even baffle you. You will feel that you did everything right, that you made a strong case, and that your proposal was sound and fit the guidelines offered by the foundation, — and you may still not get the grant. Do not despair, and do not be afraid to knock on that door again in the future.

This section is made to help you understand the foundations you will be approaching for assistance and will offer some resources to get you started. The major question most not-for-profits have regarding this starting point is, "Where do I go to get started?"

# Foundation Databases

Although pricey, foundation and grant databases can be a good investment if your organization plans to apply for grants on a regular basis. A one-year subscription to a database service can garner several years' worth of contacts, if used correctly. Two of the most notable databases available on the market today are those offered by the Foundation Center in Washington, D.C., (**www.foundationcenter.org**) and Foundation Search (**www.foundationsearch.com**). Both offer a comprehensive listing of foundations registered with the federal government and grants that have been awarded over the last decade.

**The Foundation Center**SM (**www.foundationcenter.org**): Located in Washington, D.C., it has established itself as a leading authority on U.S. philanthropies since its inception in 1956. Offering a variety of free services and training throughout the United States and a free newsletter, *The Philanthropic News* — which sends out daily updates on the foundations and grants every not-for-profit should be aware of — it is considered one of the best places for not-for-profits to go for foundation grant information.

The Foundation Center currently maintains one of the most comprehensive databases of U.S. grant makers and their grants. Their online directory, "Foundation Directory Online," can either be purchased for individual use or used at one of the many free regional libraries / learning centers available across the country. To find a library near you that offers the free service, check out the center's Web site for a state-by-state listing.

For organizations that want to subscribe to the online directory, there are several levels of service available, ranging in price from $195 per year to more than $1,200. The basic service, which is available free of charge at the learning centers discussed earlier, includes information on the top 10,000 foundations in the nation, with 11 searchable keyword fields. The Professional level service is more comprehensive and features more than 96,000 foundation and grant entries, with the capability of viewing foundations' Federal 990s and analyzing their giving trends over the past year or more.

**Foundation Search (www.foundationsearch.com):** For those wishing to expand their search to include foundation grants offered through Canadian and other worldwide foundations, Foundation Search may be the answer. Privately owned and operated by a Canadian corporation since 1988, Foundation Search is as comprehensive as the Foundation Center's Online Directory. It offers a few extra benefits, including a separate database for offshore foundations, 990 files for all subscription levels, comprehensive giving trend graphs, and a separate database. The database offers a comprehensive list of brand-new foundations as soon as they register with the federal government, which may give a not-for-profit organization the edge in applying for funding before anyone else even knows the foundation exists.

Foundation Search boasts more than 120,000 foundation listings in its database and can search for either foundations or grants by type, region, interest area, recipient, level, size, or by using any number of other criteria available.

Another bonus offered by Foundation Search is their other directory, "Big Online," the only North American Database featuring corporate, foundation, and government grant-making opportunities and information.

**The Chronicle of Philanthropy$^{SM}$: The Newspaper of the Nonprofit World (http://philanthropy.com):** This is a wonderful resource for the latest not-for-profit information. *The Chronicle of Philanthropy* is a biweekly newspaper available online and in a print edition that is geared toward charity leaders, fundraisers, grant makers, and the entire community of people involved in philanthropic enterprises.

The many features of the chronicle include philanthropic news, guides to grants, information on managing not-for-profit organizations, and many other services. Grant seekers searching for financial support in nearly every field of the not-for-profit world can likely find organizations, Web sites, and publications that can assist them in their quest. Whether you are searching for funding for a faith-based, arts, or community garden organization, there is bound to be a resource out there to suit your needs. The best place to start is with one of the above-mentioned databases. They can point you in the right direction.

Grant seekers looking for money for faith-based causes and projects can consider looking at online directories devoted to helping such organizations find the grant money they need. Several examples of such directories are:

- Christian Foundation Grants (**www.christianfoundationgrants. com**) is an online directory that features a 73,000-plus listing of foundations that have supported faith-based causes in the past.

- Christian Grants (**www.christiangrants.com**) also offers a comprehensive database and some free grant writing training.

- The Foundation for Jewish Philanthropies (**www.jewishphilan-thropies.org/index.html**) manages hundreds of individual endowment funds

Grant seekers looking for monies for the arts have a large number of options they can turn to begin their search. One of the best arts-related directories is:

**The New York Foundation for the Arts (www.nyfa.org)**: The NYFA is a good place to start your search for an arts grant. They claim to have "the most extensive national directory of awards, services, and publications for artists. Listings include over 4,200 arts organizations, 2,900 award programs, 4,200 service programs, and 900 publications for individual artists across the country. More programs are added every day."

You can also consider turning to a regional directory to help you in your search. A great example of a regional directory is:

**The Donors Forum (www.donorsforum.org)**: There are hundreds of smaller databases available for every state, region, and even interest area; some smaller ones are even available for free. A good example of a state-based, not-for-profit assistance center is the Donors Forum in Illinois. The Donors Forum is an excellent source of information regarding philanthropy in Illinois. They maintain a comprehensive library and database for use by grant seekers and grant makers. Many states throughout the United States have similar organizations.

Whether you begin your search at the Foundation Center, Foundation Search, or the Chronicle of Philanthropy, you will come across ads for foundation directories. Inexpensive, easy-to-use foundation directories can be a good way to obtain basic information on foundations in your interest area. Once you locate a foundation that may match your needs through a directory, you can get the more specific information from the foundation itself.

Foundation directories, in print or CD-ROM format, can cost anywhere from $30 to $400, depending on their size and the amount of information offered. It might be a good investment if you do not have access to an organization like the Donors Forum.

Another option is to use a print directory in your search. One of the biggest drawbacks to using a print directory is the fact that many are outdated before they ever hit bookstore shelves. In the time it takes the book's writer and editor to compile the information and have it printed in a readable, user-friendly guide, the information is often old. Foundations move, change their telephone numbers, hire new contact personnel, and even change their entire focus and giving methods, rendering the information in the directories of little or no use. They are useful, though, if you are willing to take the extra time necessary to research the foundations further and to ensure that the contact and application information is current.

The Internet is the place where you will begin any grant search. This is a good place to start your search, but be aware that not every foundation is present in cyberspace — many smaller family foundations have no Web presence at all. Still, the Internet is a good place to begin. Depending on your Web searching abilities, the Internet can offer comprehensive results quickly and at no cost. Another warning about using the Internet to search for grants: The results may be more satisfying if you search for information on specific foundations than if you merely type the words "grants" or "foundations" into your search engine.

To search for information in your geographic area, be sure to enter specific keywords to help focus the search; broad searches are a waste of time and energy. For example, instead of searching educational grants, try entering "grants for reading tutors in Boise, Idaho," or "building grants for church construction available in Pennsylvania" into the search engine.

Once you have located a foundation that looks promising, check out its Web site; investigate the programs and organizations they have already funded.

In addition to searching for funding agencies or checking out ones you have already discovered, the Web offers an unlimited amount of free resources and even smaller directories that can help you locate the grants.

As you begin to employ any of the services noted above, you may be beginning a database of your own. Think about the information you have compiled already as you begin your quest for a foundation grant. You have all the information put together about your organization; you have resources that you will employ to assist you in getting information about foundations; and you are starting to pile up the information on foundations themselves.

Fortunately, there is computer software available to help you manage this information for grant seekers of all levels of experience. The software can help you manage all the information you compile, assist with time management during your quest for grants, and help you to even write the grant. Because most grant applications ask for much of the same information, the grant writing software can help construct a solid proposal in a minimum amount of time. A drawback is that your proposal might sound ordinary; the upside of this grant software is everything the software can do for you. The software can become your personal database to track the foundations you have identified.

As you become more involved with the world of philanthropy, you may be faced with deciding which grant-writing software is right for you. The differences, strengths, and weaknesses of these packaged software tools is something you may want to consider as you look into your needs — present and future.

Here is a list of some popular grant writing software. Like all fundraising software, your organizational needs may best determine what is right for you:

- ProposalMaster™ (Sant Corporation)
- GrantWave (Mindcoast)

Using search databases and grant writing software can make your grant search and application process easier. Take your time to research these options and find the best one for you. You may find a database or software that is not mentioned here — and by all means, use those resources. Although the resources mentioned here are some of the more popular, these are not the only resources available to you. Find what works with your organization and stick with it.

# Section 3

## Whom Do You Ask? Why and How Do You Ask Them for Funding?

The mission of this section is to take you to the point of making your initial query to potential funders. Here we will begin to fine-tune your search process. At this point, you should have completed these steps:

- Developed a mission statement
- Developed a vision statement
- Written a history of your organization
- Put together a strategic plan
- Made an organizational assessment of needs
- Examined why foundations give
- Explored the types of grants that may be available to you

You are now fairly well-armed with the information you need to pinpoint your search.

The chapters in this section will more precisely explore how to go about discovering who gives to whom. What do they support? What kind of support is given? How much are they likely to give? What, if anything, are they asking for in return? When do they give? We will begin a basic fundraising calendar that will assist in tracking when proposals are due. The calendar will also come into play as grants are awarded, as you will need to track follow-up information that foundations will require.

Operating under the principle that it is better to "measure twice and cut once," we will go back again and look at your needs before that initial letter of inquiry is written. It is time to put some fundable needs on paper. While doing this, it is most important that the seeker keep the organization's mission in mind. If a need does not fit within the mission, do not cling to it — even if funding might be available for it.

At this point, it is wise to sit down with some close stakeholders, such as an organizational board of directors, to explain the plan of action. Do any stakeholders know anyone at the targeted foundation? How might the stakeholders respond if presented a similar proposal?

As the seeker hones ideas before the stakeholders, he or she will sharpen the needs statement. In this section, we will begin to write the proposal by defining what it is the seeker will be asking for. The goal here is to chisel out the one- or two-sentence request.

At the close of this section, we will learn how to write the initial query letter and discuss ways to present your organization in the best possible light. In grant writing, you may never get a second chance to make a good first impression. The techniques shown in this section will help your organization make an excellent first impression.

# Chapter 12

## Research, Research, and More Research

We closed the last section by looking at general resources that can help set you in the right direction in your quest for a foundation grant. In this chapter, we will get a bit more specific in this quest. We will look at some of the ways foundations identify their giving trends and preferences, and we will present a formalized strategy for identifying just the right foundation(s) to approach with your initial letter of inquiry.

As we saw in the last chapter, there are many resources available to look for funding sources. There are databases for sale, online resources, libraries, publications, and programs put out by organizations similar to yours. You could make a full-time job out of combing through all this information as you look for the perfect foundation. You are likely to identify at least one good candidate in any one of the sources you look into. So, take the first step: Choose a path, and take it. Let us return to our fictional community garden, Amicitia Community Gardens, to follow the path that Rose took.

Rose, our director of Amicitia Community Gardens, located the XYZ Foundation by researching other community gardens. She visited various community garden Web sites and, as she explored, she read many Web pages that identified the supporters of organizations that were much like hers. In doing so, she noticed that the XYZ Foundation supported several gardens that were located in her state, and she made a note of that. She also noted several other foundations that she believed to be possible candidates.

Rose came across a promising foundation that supported a garden in a nearby community. As she looked into it, however, she discovered that the foundation supported organizations that were in that specific community. It would be a waste of her time to pursue a grant from this foundation.

Later, Rose came across another foundation that supported a co-op farm located just outside her city, but as she looked further into their support, she discovered that the foundation limits its support to organizations in rural communities. She marked that one off her list.

Rose then came across the XYZ Foundation during her Web search. She clicked on their Web site, and found:

*The XYZ Foundation began its charitable giving program in 1967. The Foundation grew out of the success of the Zander Family Farm near Westview and their passionate belief in agricultural education and research, as well as their enduring belief in community service.*

*The Zander Family Farm's success has made the XYZ Foundation, and its support of education and creative programs that benefit the Westview community, possible.*

*The XYZ Foundation supports proposals that mirror the foundation's belief in community service and contribute to an organization's mission and service while offering leadership in the areas of agriculture, education, and human services.*

*The XYZ Foundation Inc. is a private philanthropic foundation created by Samuel Zander and his family. It became active after Samuel Zander's death in 1966.*

*The Zander Foundation's vision is to improve the quality of life in rural and urban communities by promoting healthy lifestyles and education. The foundation they created works to guarantee that their ideals will benefit many more in generations to come.*

*The XYZ Foundation supports a variety of charitable causes in Westview and the surrounding tri-state region, including agricultural programs, environmental projects, higher education, and public schools.*

Rose thought this sounded quite promising, noting that there were a number of needs identified in Amicitia Gardens' strategic plan that she could consider submitting in a proposal to the XYZ Foundation for support.

She continued to explore the XYZ Foundation's Web site, investigating the programs that they were involved in:

## Programs

*Zander Farms: Started by Samuel Zander in 1919, this 120-acre working organic farm is a popular destination for school children throughout the region. The farm is designated as one of the only certified organic and biodynamic farms in the region and produces a wide variety of fruits, vegetables, and other food items. The farm also has more than 300 chickens, 30 pigs, and 15 cows. The farm is an important education and research facility for sustainable agriculture and alternative crops, and features an apple orchard where ten varieties of apples are grown. Zander Farms regularly schedules workshops on organic farming and food production.*

*Zander Farm Biodynamic Research Center helps agricultural producers, backyard gardeners, and their communities nurture the biodynamic movement in the region through education, research, and development.*

*Zander Farms Urban Education Program is designed to bring the idea of sustainable urban farming and gardening to young and old alike in Westview and the tri-state region. The program focuses on biodynamic organic farming and gardening, sustainable agriculture, and nutrition through outdoor experiential education.*

The programs that this foundation supports are very similar to the program that Amicitia Community Gardens is focused on creating. This is an important aspect of a foundation. During a grant search, you should always look at the programs that the foundation supported in the past. These past programs will give you the opportunity to see if your organization and a particular foundation will be good partners.

Based on this information, Rose believed that Amicitia Community Gardens and the XYZ Foundation would work together nicely. Now, she will investigate their site further to see what grants they offer. She saw that there was a button linked to a "Grants" page, and she clicked it:

## Grants

*The XYZ Foundation provides funds to organizations in Westview and the tri-state area that are classified as public charities by the Internal Revenue Service and are exempt from tax. The Foundation gives high priority to proposals that focus on these three areas:*

   *\* **Agriculture**, notably the teaching and study of organic biodynamic agricultural practices, with particular emphasis on horticulture*

\* **Education**, *particularly programs of broad impact in agriculture and social sciences*

\* **Ecology**, *with particular emphasis placed on partnerships aimed at sustainability, recycling, and renewable resources.*

*In all programs, the XYZ Foundation stresses the importance of interdisciplinary approaches and organizational collaboration.*

*The Foundation supports projects that are innovative and make new contributions in the fields of education and horticulture. The Foundation encourages matching grants of equal or greater size, and contributes considerably to an organization's mission and service to its stakeholders.*

*The majority of grant proposals are for program funding. The Foundation places a low priority on support for operating expenses. Inquire with the Foundation prior to the beginning of a project.*

Upon reading the information on what types of organizations the foundation supports, Rose decided to download its guidelines:

# XYZ CHARITABLE FOUNDATION GRANT GUIDELINES

Mr. Samuel Zander Jr., President

Box 432

Blanton, IN 44444

*We fund or provide funds only to organizations operating in the states of Indiana, Illinois, and Michigan that are both exempt from taxation under the Internal Revenue Code (IRC) & 501(c)(3) and are classified as a "public charity" under IRC 509(a)(1) or (2), and Type I, Type II, and "functionally integrated" Type III, supporting organizations under IRC 509(a)(3) as described in IRC 170(c)(1).*

*FUNDS WILL NOT BE AWARDED TO: any organization whose mission is to carry out propaganda, influence public election, attempt religious promotion, or influence legislation. The XYZ Foundation does not award monies in the form of a loan.*

Rose stopped reading at this point and wondered what all this meant. She wondered, primarily, about all of those codes. "Is Amicitia Community Gardens classified as a 'public charity' under any of these codes?" she wondered. Rose was certain that her organization was classified as a 501(c) (3) organization. She knew that to be a not-for-profit organization, Amicitia Community Gardens had to register as such with the IRS after incorporating in her state. Rose wondered, though, about all those other codes that were mentioned in the guidelines.

Rose did more research and discovered that the IRC codes that were further mentioned in the XYZ Foundation guidelines are sub-classifications of charitable organizations. She learned that all 501(c) (3) organizations are further categorized as one of five types under IRC 509(a). It just so happened that Amicitia Community Gardens is recognized as 509(a) (1). This simply means that Amicitia Community Gardens is a publicly supported charity. It also means that Rose can continue in her quest for a grant from the XYZ Foundation.

## Grant Seeking Tip

If you come across tax codes that you are not sure of during your research, search **www.irs.gov**. It is always best to be certain of your status before pursuing the grant.

Rose returned to the guidelines of the XYZ Foundation and continued to read about the objectives and priorities of the foundation. She also found information on the stipulations of the grant amount:

*The majority of grants awarded are less than $50,000. It is possible for a grant to be awarded in an amount greater than $50,000, but the proposal must highly reflect the priorities of the community served.*

At this point, Rose figured that Amicitia Community Gardens' focus applied to the focus of the XYZ Foundation and that the funding was within the amounts she would be asking for. Rose now has to explore the XYZ Foundation's application process. She carefully read through the grant application guidelines:

# GRANT APPLICATION GUIDELINES – THE XYZ FOUNDATION

1. ***Need:*** *Define proposed project for funding. It is necessary that a case is made for the proposed project that shows why it is needed and how it meets the needs of the organization. It must be clear how the project fits within the overall mission and vision of the applicant organization. It is vital that this statement of need is brief and clear.*

2. ***Qualifications:*** *Applicant must define organizational history and explain how the organization is qualified to undertake the proposed project. Applicant must present proof of organizational experience, expertise, and ability to manage proposed project.*

3. ***Financial Ability:*** *Applicant organization must present proof of financial stability, ability, and sound practice. Organization must present a view of the organizational budget in relation to the proposed project budget. Definition must also be given of overall organizational development plan with particular emphasis placed on project sustainability after the grant period. It is vital that this statement of financial ability be accurate.*

4. ***Partnerships:*** *Cooperative projects and ventures, when appropriate, will often strengthen an application. If a collaborative project is proposed, the role of each organization must be defined. The application must also define the benefit to each of the organizations in the partnership.*

5. **Assessment:** *Application must contain a defined assessment strategy that spells out the method to be employed to measure the effectiveness of the project following the grant period.*

6. ***Capacity Building:*** *Definition should be given as to how the proposed project will help the applicant organization grow. Simply proving that the organization will provide sustainability for the project is not enough.*

After reading the application guidelines, Rose felt good about her ability to put together a strong grant proposal. She had done her research, and she had most, if not all, the information the XYZ Foundation was asking for. There were, however, a few more pieces of information Rose needed before she proceeded:

# GRANT APPLICATION PROCESS

1. ***Submissions:*** *Organizations considering submitting proposals to the XYZ Foundation should contact us regarding our priorities, the process for submitting a proposal, and the funding schedule well in advance of beginning the project. The board of directors of the XYZ Foundation meets quarterly, although funding applications are not reviewed at every meeting. Inquiries should be submitted in writing and sent to the address specified in the guidelines. Approved inquiries and applications are reviewed within one to three months of receipt.*

2. ***Funding Allocations****: Awarded funds are disbursed four times a year: April, July, October, and December. Project proposals must note when funds are required.*

3. ***Re-application****: Applications from organizations that have had proposals reviewed (whether accepted or rejected) within the preceding 12 months will not be accepted.*

### GRANT APPLICATIONS THAT ARE INCOMPLETE WILL NOT BE CONSIDERED.

Rose now felt that she had everything she needed to proceed in her quest. She still had considerable work to do, but she had taken a huge step forward. She knew that she now had to identify a project proposal that Amicitia Community Gardens could submit to the XYZ Foundation.

She has already put together most of the information she will need for this proposal. If you have prepared this information while reading this book up to this point, you also have most of the information you need. The preparatory work that has been done before we came across the XYZ Foundation is in the form of:

- Mission statement
- Visions statement
- Account of the organization's history
- Strategic plan
- Assessment plan

It is important to compare the preparation for the grant requirements that the XYZ Foundation put forth to the guidelines stated by the XYZ Foundation. The guidelines are quite standard. Some foundations will have application forms, while others — like the XYZ Foundation — will specify the information that should be included. For the most part, much of the information requested is similar from foundation to foundation.

Look at the organizational preparation you have already taken care of and compare it to what is required in the foundation guidelines: Most of the work needed to put a grant proposal together is already done. Rose felt she had done solid preparatory work. She had put together quite a bit of information. She also felt that before she went any further, she had to do a better job of organizing the information into an effective proposal.

## CASE STUDY: ROBERT L. MYERS, PH.D.

Thomas Jefferson Agricultural Institute
601 W. Nifong Blvd., Ste. 1d
Columbia, MO 65203
Phone: 573-441-2740
**www.jeffersoninstitute.org**

Thomas Jefferson Agricultural Institute is a 501(c) (3) nonprofit agriculture education and research center that has been in existence for 11 years. I have been seeking and writing foundation grants for the Institute for 11 years.

I generally write grants for specific projects, but have also applied to foundations for general support funds (hard to get) and for capital projects. I develop the proposal idea, research the relevant foundations, write the proposal, and submit it.

Our foundation funding has varied tremendously, from a high of about $1.5 million to below $200,000 in a year. We have received about an equal amount of funding in government grants over time and have generally offset the poor years in foundation funding with higher levels of government grants. Our most common requests to foundations are for education projects, but we have also sought capital funding and, more recently, some general support funding.

I think a compelling grant proposal is one that is in line with the funder's goals; is written to provide the information they ask for; is novel enough for the funder to get excited about; and has very tangible benefits that can occur in the near future. When I am researching foundations, I look for ones that fund our type of project or organization that give grants in the size range we are looking for, and that give out at least a moderate number of grants at that funding level. Our best success with foundations is when we have had a personal relationship with a foundation officer before getting funded. Our second-best success rate has come from seeking capital gifts on a one-time basis; it seems a lot of foundations are hesitant to get involved in project funding, at least the type we do.

I have applied to about 40 different foundations and had grants from about 10 of them. Some good advice I had with foundations was to apply to a lot of different foundations because the success rate is low. However, if you get a personal meeting with a foundation officer, I think the success rate goes from single digits up to 20-30 percent. I have found, in general, it is easier to get a meeting before submitting a proposal. For the foundation arm of a large company, if you can find a contact who knows a senior at that company, that can help you get your foot in the door. You have got to find a way to be different from the hundreds of other applications they are getting.

# Chapter 13

## Organization and Scheduling Techniques

Now that all the prepared information is gathered, it is time to begin a foundation search. Organization of this material is vital to being successful. All these materials should be saved on your computer and to a backup device; there should also be a hard copy stored in a file cabinet. It is a good idea to have a file for each document with any notes on how that document was created, and is also beneficial to have a folder for each of the foundations you wish to apply to. This organization technique will not only keep you organized, but will also save you time when you get ready to submit your proposal.

### Grant $eeking Tip

Your grant files should contain hard copies of all your organizational information. These files will contain your mission and vision statements, long-term strategic plan, organizational history, organizational articles of incorporation, IRS letter of not-for-profit status, IRS 990s, and audited financial statements. If you are an individual seeking foundation grants, your files should contain as much of this information as you can put together.

The primary reason for having all this material on file is so it is available when needed for a proposal. Many of these documents are standard attachments added to most foundation proposals. Often, you will be required to add multiple copies of some of these documents to your proposal, so it is a good idea to have multiple copies already printed and filed — it is much easier to put the final proposal package together when you have all this information on hand.

Many of the larger foundations, especially the corporate foundations, will require you to file your proposal electronically, so it is good to be prepared to respond in this manner, as well. In the case of electronic proposals, you will probably be instructed as to which format the file should be submitted in. You will download an application to fill out, or you will follow the guidelines — similar to the guidelines of the XYZ Foundation — and submit your proposal in whatever file form they request. If you are prepared with files saved in every format, you can expedite this process.

# Making a Grant-seeking Calendar

If you have not already started a grant-seeking calendar, now would be a good time to get one started. This will become a valuable tool. As you make more grant queries and identify more foundations to approach, the dates pertaining to inquiry deadlines, final proposal deadlines, decisions, and grant periods will become such that keeping track of them in your personal date book is not advisable. Ideally, you will have so much grant activity going on that these dates will crowd out everything else in your calendar.

Starting a grant-seeking calendar is even more vital if you work in an organization with a large number of employees and, even moreso, if you are an organization with numerous departments. These are the benefits of having a grant-seeking calendar:

- It will keep everyone informed and up-to-date on the grant-seeking process
- It will identify funding avenues and the deadlines associated with those avenues
- It will identify how funding is found for priority projects.

Let us take a look at the work Rose did in preparing Amicitia Community Gardens' grant-seeking calendar. She has already identified numerous projects that require funding assistance, taken directly from the long-term strategic plan she and her staff put together. She has organized grant-seeking for near-future projects and projects she hopes to begin in three years. Each of the projects in the strategic plan are associated with various departments within the organization, and all of these projects should be a part of the overall grant-seeking calendar.

Before we make a grant-seeking calendar, it is a good idea to put some information together on the proposed projects for the next three years. Making a flow sheet allows you to put specific details of each of the proposed projects in a chart. This is a document that will simplify the making of the grant-seeking calendar.

The flow sheet should comprise:

- Title of project
- Project schedule
- Estimated project cost
- All potential funding sources

It is important to identify all potential funding, even if it is not from a foundation. By doing this, the flow sheet will indicate which programs would benefit more from a grant search. When putting together the potential funding information, ask these questions:

- Is state or federal funding available for any of these projects?
- Do we have individuals who may be interested in supporting any of the projects?
- Do we have a business that may like sponsoring a certain project?
- Can we seek partial funding for any of the projects from foundations while balancing the funding out through any of the above sources?

## Grant Seeking Tip

To begin your grant-seeking calendar, list the projects and programs from your flow sheet that you have identified as being grant-worthy, followed by an ideal schedule. As you identify foundations that may fund the noted projects and programs, match the foundation dates to the schedule you have identified for your projects and programs, and note that information in the grant-seeking calendar.

Rose prepared a flow sheet with all this information. She began to have an idea as to the number of projects she would need foundation funding for. Rose knew from experience that any grant-seeking calendar she created should also include all grant activities the organization was involved in, and all the federal and state granting agencies that Amicitia Community Gardens planned on applying to.

## Grant Seeking Tip

If you come across a foundation that accepts applications year-round and sets no specific deadlines, follow the schedule you set for yourself in your program and project schedule. Set a deadline for yourself and stick to it.

Now that Rose has her flow sheet of organizational plans for the next three years, she can use this sheet to guide her in the construction of her calendar. She has decided to make a 24-month calendar; her task now is to merge her flow sheet into her calendar.

Rose started by identifying the project information because all project funds need to be obtained prior to the beginning of the program. She had identified potential project funders from all her foundation research, and, considering all the deadlines, she started to enter that information on her calendar. She was mindful that her schedule allowed plenty of preparation time for each potential proposal.

| Deadline | Scheduled Activity | Affected Organizational Project |
|---|---|---|
| March 1, 2008 | Write intent letter to Ferber Foundation due March 5, 2008 | $5,000 Gardeners in Schools |
| March 1, 2008 | Begin to prepare XYZ Foundation final report due March 14 | "Grow the Community" |
| March 3, 2008 | Begin to prepare Westview CityGreen grant final draft due March 21 | Amicitia Community Gardens operating expense $15,000 |
| March 5, 2008 | Bastion Fund decision day! | "How Green Our Valley" $10,000 |
| March 5, 2008 | Ferber Foundation Intent Letter due | $5,000 Gardeners in Schools |
| March 8, 2008 | Final draft of State Humanities Council grant completed for March 15 due date | $10,000 Gardeners in Schools '09 – '10 |
| March 14, 2008 | XYZ Foundation final report due | "Grow the Community" |
| March 15, 2008 | State Humanities Council grant due | $10,000 Gardeners in the Schools '09 - '10 |
| March 18, 2008 | Ferber Foundation grant drafted | $5,000 Gardeners in Schools |
| March 21, 2008 | Westview CityGreen grant due | Amicitia Community Gardens operating expenses $15,000 |
| March 23, 2008 | Draft Robbins Foundation final report due April 7 | PV Newsletter support |

| Deadline | Scheduled Activity | Affected Organizational Project |
| --- | --- | --- |
| March 26, 2008 | Ferber Foundation grant due | $5,000 Gardeners in Schools 2010 |
| March 26, 2008 | State Humanities Council site visit | Gardeners in Schools, '09 – '10 |
| Deadline | Foundation Name and Document Due | Affected Organizational Project |
| March 1, 2008 | Ferber Foundation intent letter due | $5,000 Gardeners in Schools |
| March 1, 2008 | XYZ Foundation final report due | "Grow the Community" |
| March 3, 2008 | Westview CityGreen grant due | Amicitia Community Gardens operating expense $15,000 |
| March 5, 2008 | Bastion Fund decision day! | "How Green Our Valley" $10,000 |
| March 8, 2008 | State Humanities Council grant due | $10,000 Gardeners in Schools '09 – '10 |
| March 15, 2008 | Write thank-you letter to XYZ Foundation for supporting "Grow the Community" | |
| March 18, 2008 | Ferber Foundation grant drafted | $5,000 Gardeners in Schools |
| March 18, 2008 | Clabber Foundation intent letter due | $7,500 Farmers' Market stall rent support, 2010 |
| March 23, 2008 | Letter of collaboration signed with City of Westview | "Farm in the Park" |
| March 23, 2008 | Robbins Foundation final report due | PV Newsletter support |
| March 26, 2008 | Ferber Foundation grant due | $5,000 Gardeners in Schools 2010 |
| March 26, 2008 | State Humanities Council site visit | Gardeners in Schools, '09 – '10 |

This is just one month from Rose's 24-month grant calendar. If you get the impression that it is a great deal of work, you are correct. It is not absolutely necessary to put a grant-seeking calendar together; however, once you have begun this grant-seeking process, you will discover how much easier your life can be if you are prepared.

Note the variety of information that Rose's calendar contains, from letters of intent to thank-you letters. She has noted dates when grants are due and when final reports should be completed. Also, note that she entered other information that was important to an approaching grant, such as getting a letter of collaboration signed. The grant-seeking calendar included information pertaining to foundation grants, as well as state and local grants. She entered information regarding corporate support, as well. It is important that your calendar is as detailed as possible so you and those that work with you can get a complete a picture of your activities. Remember to keep your calendar up-to-date.

# Chapter 14

## Going Back to Your Strategic Plan

We will now go back to the time when Rose was just beginning to think about her first foundation grant — back when she had just decided that the XYZ Foundation might be a good fit for Amicitia Community Gardens, and Amicitia Community Gardens would be a good fit for the XYZ Foundation. We will look at Rose's strategic plan and determine which points need funding and which do not.

When you make your grant-seeking calendar, you will want to re-examine the needs that you outlined in your strategic plan, illustrated in the form of objectives and activities. Remember, the objectives from your plan were good projects to consider for foundation grants because they were SMART — specific, measurable, achievable, realistic, and timely. Activities have those same qualities and, therefore, are easily assessed.

Now let us look at Amicitia Community Gardens' long-term strategic plan to mine it for needs that may prove to need foundation funding. Below are the objectives and activities from the Amicitia Community Gardens' strategic plan.

**Notice what has been crossed out from the strategic plan:**

## *Goal 1*

*To assist families in growing food for themselves*

## Objectives

- To increase the number of family memberships in ACG by 15 percent annually over the next three years

- To increase professional assistance available to families for the purpose of developing their own property or community garden plot by 15 percent annually over the next three years

- To increase seed stock available to families by 50 percent

- To improve communication between families involved in ACG programs for a more open exchange of ideas and information

## Activities

- Expand ACG community information program in neighborhood schools, neighborhood associations, churches, and other community-based institutions

- ~~Partner with community colleges throughout the area to provide internships for students studying agriculture, horticulture, and landscaping~~

- Increase seed saving initiative by 50 percent to make greater seed stack available

- Expand organizational Web site to include family forum area for use by neighborhood family gardeners

## Goal 2

*To further the development of the Community Garden Initiative*

### Objectives

- To have at least one community garden in each precinct of the city within the next three years

- To have a part-time Gardening Associate working at each of neighborhood's community gardens within the next three years

- To begin seed stores associated with each community garden

- To increase advocacy efforts on behalf of community gardens

### Activities

- Begin three new community gardens in different city precincts per year for the next three years

- Increase funding available to hire and train nine part-time Gardening Associates over the next three years

- ~~Recruit volunteers associated with each of the city's community gardens to begin seed saving and storage programs~~

- ACG staff will expand advocacy of community gardening by lobbying city to use space in three central city parks as "showcase" community gardens within the next three years

## *Goal 3*

*To assist ACG member gardeners interested in the commercial options of gardening*

## Objectives

- Make professional assistance available to gardeners interested in learning basic small business practices

- Make $100,000 in small business start-up grants available to community and family gardeners over the next three years

- Begin two new community co-op farmers' markets on the city's south and west side over the next two years

- Organize online seed sales initiative over the next year

## Activities

- ~~Partner with community colleges to help make small business classes such as basic bookkeeping and accounting available to ACG members at a reduced rate~~

- Increase fundraising efforts to make $100,000 in grants available for small business development among member gardeners

- Procure space for community co-op farmers' markets on south-side within ten months and west-side over the next 24 months

- Develop Web site space for the online seed sales initiative

## Goal 4

*Expand ACG educational initiatives*

## Objectives

- Establish Gardener Green Clubs in city public schools

- Establish community gardening classes in community colleges

- Offer community gardening workshops through city programs

## Activities

- Begin Green Garden Clubs in 15 public schools each year for the next three years

- Begin Green Garden Clubs in seven of the city's private schools each year for the next three years

- Develop curriculum for community gardening classes in community colleges over the year for class implementation within two years

- Develop curriculum for community gardening workshops to offer through city parks over the next year, with ten offerings available at six parks within the next two years

The plan above outlines only the projects that need grant funding. Notice the activities that are crossed out: These activities either do not need grant funding, or other funding has already been provided for them.

Rose identified all these objectives and activities as needs. At this point, the task is not identifying needs, but prioritizing them. In Chapter 7, Rose identified a high-priority need. She identified the need to have at least one community garden in each precinct of the city within the next three years as a wide-reaching objective. She decided this project was to be the focus of her first foundation grant proposal to the XYZ Foundation.

Rose went through her strategic plan carefully and saw how fulfilling this objective would affect many of the other objectives and activities of her organization. Having a community garden in every precinct of the city would make a stronger case for a partnership with the community college and with the public schools, and it would help the organization reach their family membership goals. Having more gardens would make more seed stock available, and its produce would be available for sale at the farmers' market.

As Rose considered the impact of a garden in every city precinct, she also wondered what needs would have to be filled because of this growth. She went through her list again. She would definitely have to improve the organization's communications system; this would mean expansion of the organizational Web site would be necessary sooner. She would certainly have to consider adding additional part-time gardening associates to her staff, which might require additional training. Rose wondered if she should present these needs to the XYZ Foundation, as they could necessitate further funding. "Would the funding come from other grants, donations, or sponsorship?" Rose wondered. She began to look at it all like a big puzzle.

When Rose began to look for foundation funding, she focused on the essential elements of operating her not-for-profit business. She did not develop her mission statement as a means to go out and look for funding; rather, she developed her mission statement to define Amicitia Community Gardens for herself and all of her stakeholders. Now she is excited as she works toward achieving her organization's mission.

As you went through all of Rose's Activities in this chapter, you should notice how having a developed strategic plan came in handy. When you analyze your strategic plan, remember to prioritize your goals, objectives, and activities according to:

- Funding
  - Does this project need foundation funding?
  - Is there funding already established?

- Priority
  - Will it affect the other goals?
  - Will it assist in the completion of the other goals?

---

## CASE STUDY: MICHAEL HEYL, PUBLIC HEALTH EDUCATOR

Lincoln Lancaster County Health Department (LLCHD)
3140 N Street
Lincoln, NE 68510
**www.lincoln.ne.gov**

The LLCHD is the oldest and largest local health department in the state of Nebraska. We provide essential health services and partner with many organizations and agencies (public and private) to ensure those services are provided. The department was created in 1886, although a board of health was created in 1873.

I have been employed in public health at either the state or local level in Nebraska since 1989. In that time, securing funding through grants and foundations has been essential to the existence of the programs I have been involved with. These programs include physical activity, nutrition, safety, planning and evaluation, and employee wellness.

Most of the funding I am currently working with is state funds from the Nebraska Health and Human Services System. The largest of these is the LB 692 fund that was created when the state received a settlement from the tobacco companies in the late 1990s.

## CASE STUDY: MICHAEL HEYL, PUBLIC HEALTH EDUCATOR

We also seek and work with Community Health Endowment funds, specific just to organizations in the city of Lincoln and Lancaster County; with Centers for Disease Control funds; with private foundations such as the Robert Wood Johnson Foundation and the Kellogg Foundation; U.S. Department of Transportation programs in the Federal Highway Administration Safety Program; and Safe Kids Worldwide funding. The funds we seek can go to personnel expenditures; operating costs such as printing, rent, and transportation; and indirect costs. In the fiscal year 2008-09, my program received about $288,000 in funds from a variety of grants, of which $266,000 is LB 692 funds that are divided between four programs.

The need for the funds and the plan for allocating the funds makes for a compelling grant proposal. We have found that the better the picture we can paint about the population or community being served, the better the granting foundation relates to the need of those being served by the funding. Including socio-economic data, census tract data, past efforts by the community that were successful, as well as geographic data, helps with the application. Having a business plan on how the money will be spent, including data analysis of outcomes that are expected to occur because of the funding, is essential. Demonstrating that the program will include a diverse and well-connected group of partners is also essential, as no one organization can achieve all of its goals by itself; it takes many organizations working together to have the greatest success.

What we look for in a funder is an organization willing to partner with the department on technical assistance that assists with program development and implementation, as well as provides funds. What funders see in us is the leader in public health — not just in our community, but also recognized across the state and the country for being innovative and collaborative in our efforts.Some words of wisdom that I would relate to those who are new to seeking foundation funding is to never give up, keep plugging away, and do not be afraid to use someone else's ideas. Always attempt to relate requested funds directly to proposed outcomes.

# Chapter 15

## Going Back to Your Stakeholders

Puzzles are sometimes fun to do by yourself — but working out puzzles as a team can be an especially rewarding experience. Rose took her questions, research, and observations to her closest stakeholders to get advice.

First, Rose sat down with the people she worked with on a daily basis to get their thoughts on her decided path. Rose kept open lines of communications with her closest stakeholders, who had helped to define Amicitia Community Gardens' strategic plan, and she now asked their approval of her priorities. She explained how, if Amicitia Community Gardens were to get this funding, their work would be affected. Remember, foundations are interested in being assured that your organization is capable of handling the project you are proposing. If your proposed project is one that will over-tax your entire organization, burn out your employees, and leave your enterprise totally exhausted, it is probably not time to embark on this project.

Rose needed to know that those who handled the day-to-day activities at Amicitia Community Gardens were on board. She explained to them the consequences of the growth that this funding could have. Yes, it was a positive growth, but with it, the organization would undergo major changes.

There was considerable talk about grants at this staff meeting. Several staff members had ideas about what the priority projects should be. One member complained about the additional work this growth would bring. He made the point that the additional work would be placed on a small staff that already seemed a little overwhelmed. A few of the volunteers wondered whether this meant that they might find paid employment with the organization. There were even a few ideas as to where additional funding might come from.

The one thing everybody present agreed upon was that the most important thing was the mission of the organization. Everybody agreed that the premise of the proposal that Rose was suggesting did spring directly from the organizational mission of Amicitia Community Gardens. The team approved of the proposal, and Rose informed them that she would share all their thoughts, concerns, and opinions with the Amicitia Community Gardens Board of Directors.

By the time Rose shared her proposal plans with the Amicitia Community Gardens Board of Directors, she was more confident in her ideas. By this time, she knew that her staff was behind her. She understood the possible consequences that funding approval might bring, but she also knew and believed that her team could handle any task. She still wondered, though, about where additional funding would come from. She did not think that this proposal would come through without the promise of additional funding, but she was fairly certain that if she could show the promise — or the possibility, at least — of additional funding, then her proposal to the XYZ Foundation would be much stronger.

Rose spelled her plans out to the board of directors in much the same way that she had to her staff, and she shared her staff's thoughts with them. The board had many of the same concerns that the staff had. One board member, however, came prepared with some good news. It seems that this particular board member knew someone who was affiliated with the Westview Community Foundation who might be interested in working with Amicitia Community Gardens. He explained to Rose that it would be worth her while to contact this individual about the opportunity. He also explained that from what he had been told, this particular foundation was about to offer sizable capacity-building-grant opportunities to a number of local not-for-profits. Rose knew that because of the growth estimated from her proposal, they could qualify for a capacity-building grant.

## Grant Seeking Tip

Capacity-building grants are those that enhance the effectiveness of an organization. This means that the organization can better serve its mission.

Rose spent a good deal of time talking with her board of directors about opportunity, growth, and the importance of stakeholders that believe in the mission and vision of not-for-profit organizations. There was much discussion about community building and partnerships. Rose knew that she had an important decision to make here, and her board trusted her to make the right one. She left this meeting feeling every bit as confident in her organization as she did when she left her last staff meeting.

Rose now had the opportunity to bring two new stakeholders into her organizational circle. In the following days, she spoke with her contact at the

Westview Community Foundation, who had been expecting her call. They were eager to get Rose's proposal. Rose had asked what the proposal should contain, and she was told that the foundation was interested in funding a three-year capacity-building project. She was told that she should write an initial intent-to-apply letter. This letter would describe the capacity-building project that Amicitia Community Gardens was planning. After the acceptance of this initial intent-to-apply letter, she would be required to submit an expanded proposal outlining the capacity building project, a three-year budget for that project, the organizational long-term plan, an assessment plan, and a statement describing how this capacity-building plan will aid in the organization's growth. Rose was told that these grants would be for $20,000 a year over a three-year period, beginning in the organization's next fiscal year.

Because Rose had openly shared her ideas and plans with her stakeholders, she had received input, feedback, and valuable information. Her staff bought into her plans and pledged their commitment to organizational growth. Her board of directors responded in an equally committed fashion and assisted in the growth of the circle of stakeholders.

Rose knew the value of her stakeholders before these meetings, but it was nice to be reminded that they shared the same vision. Rose knew that when she started to see grant-funding come in, it would be vital to recognize the funder and her stakeholders.

When you begin prioritizing your projects, it is important to follow Rose's example. Always remember to:

- Seek the input of your staff members. Their support and approval of the project are essential elements in its success.

## CASE STUDY: BRAD JENSEN, EXECUTIVE DIRECTOR

Huron Pines
501 Norway Street
Grayling, MI 49738
**www.huronpines.org**

Huron Pines is a 36-year-old, not-for-profit conservation organization that serves the 11-county region of Northeast

Michigan and works to achieve its mission through projects such as river restoration, watershed management, conservation leadership, and land stewardship.

I have been seeking and writing foundation grants for program support at Huron Pines for ten years. As Executive Director of Huron Pines, I am involved in developing project ideas, contacting foundation staff, preparing proposals, making presentations, and follow-up reporting and communications.

We receive approximately $200,000 a year from foundations and $900,000 a year from government-based agencies. This is funding to support our conservation programs, and seed funding that can be used to start new projects and leverage larger amounts of dollars from some of the government agencies that support our efforts.

An effective grant proposal is one that clearly shows an unmet need and demonstrates how an applicant's approach to solving that need is worth supporting. A proposal must be able to connect people, to help them understand why what you are doing is so important. We have a well-established, multi-stakeholder process for identifying and developing good projects. By the time we apply to a foundation, our project proposal has had the support of many partners and stakeholders. Our organization will press forward with what we believe are the highest priorities and most effective programs for our area, regardless of how funding shifts from year to year in foundation (and government) programs. That means sometimes we do not fit neatly into grant program guidelines, but I think our funders recognize and appreciate how we approach building support for our projects.

As a grant seeker, what I look for in a funder is one that has an interest in our geographic area and is interested in creative approaches to solving problems. Our region has very few philanthropic groups; we have to make our program appeal to supporters outside of the area.

## CASE STUDY: BRAD JENSEN, EXECUTIVE DIRECTOR

Everyone is interested in what a given foundation's priorities/preferences are; however, nonprofits should stay focused on their mission and the needs of their communities. Develop the good idea first; do not stray from it just to try to impress potential funders by being what they want. Do not give up on pushing your well-thought out proposal. If the idea is good and it meets a real need, it will eventually be  funded. And, of course, volunteers and staff involved with nonprofit organizations should never forget how valuable their work is — and the potential impact they have on their communities.

# Chapter 16

## Matching Your Needs to the Foundation's Priorities

Prior to learning about this capacity building grant, Rose had decided to approach the XYZ Foundation about assisting Amicitia Community Gardens in fulfilling the objective of having a garden in each of the city's precincts within the next three years. This, she had decided, was a primary organizational objective. Things had changed, though. She could still ask the XYZ Foundation to fund this project, but she also thought the project was a good fit for the capacity-building grant.

If Rose decided to propose having a community garden in every precinct to the Westview Community Foundation, she needed to rethink her proposal to the XYZ Foundation. She looked at the XYZ Foundation Guidelines:

*The XYZ Foundation provides funds to organizations in Westview and the tri-state area that are exempt from tax and classified as public charities by the Internal Revenue Service, giving highest priority to proposals for funding in three areas:*

> \* ***Agriculture***, *notably the teaching and study of organic biodynamic agricultural practices, with particular emphasis on horticulture*

> \* ***Education***, *particularly programs of broad impact in agriculture and social sciences*

> \* ***Ecology***, *with particular emphasis placed on partnerships aimed at sustainability, recycling, and renewable resources*

Rose knew from her discussions with staff that it would be crucial to increase the number of gardening associates on staff if the number of community gardens grew. She also knew that because they had plans to partner with the public schools and the community college system, having gardening associates would be an important part of the organization's educational initiatives. Rose made her decision. The proposal to the XYZ Foundation would be to hire and train nine part-time gardening associates over the next three years. This came directly from Amicitia Community Gardens' organizational plan, tied to the organization's mission. It was also directly tied to the funding priorities of the foundation, as they put a high priority on agriculture and education.

Rose knew that while she had a plan for the Westview Community Foundation and the XYZ Foundation, she was also going to need to expand her organization's communications ability. This meant that they needed to increase the capabilities of Amicitia Community Gardens' Web site and increase the newsletter's reach. This would take funding.

Rose considered making the communications expansion a part of one of the proposals she already had in the works. She also considered making it a part of another grant.

When Rose was doing her research on foundations, she made note of a foundation associated with the daily newspaper in Westview. The Herald Corporation owned a number of newspapers, radio, and television stations across the country. This corporation also created a foundation named the Herald Foundation. The Herald Foundation focused on providing funding to other organizations with goals to improve their communications initiatives. Rose explored the foundation's Web site and was happy to learn that she had a month before the next foundation deadline and could apply for a grant electronically. She had a week to put together an intent-to-apply letter.

Rose now had her work cut out for her. In the coming weeks, she needed to write a letter of inquiry to the XYZ Foundation, and intent-to-apply letters to the Westview Community Foundation and the Herald Foundation.

Rose's letter of inquiry to the XYZ Foundation followed the directive of the foundation guidelines that stated, "Organizations considering submitting proposals to the XYZ Foundation should make inquiries about our priorities, the application process, and funding schedule well before the beginning of the project." Rose's inquiry to the XYZ Foundation was to determine whether her proposal to hire and train nine gardening associates over the next three years would be in line with their priorities.

Rose's intent-to-apply letter to the Westview Community Foundation followed the directive of her contact at the foundation. She intended to write a proposal to the foundation that would meet Amicitia Community Gardens' objective of having a community garden in every precinct within the next three years.

Rose's intent-to-apply letter that was to be filed electronically to the Herald Foundation was to request funds to expand Amicitia Community Gardens' communications abilities. The funding would allow them to grow their Web site and increase the size and scope of their newsletter.

Rose felt good about her plan thus far: She felt as though she had covered all the bases and was hitting her stride. She had a good feeling about where Amicitia Community Gardens was heading. She felt as though she understood what the foundations required of her organization. And she believed that she had boiled her needs statements down to simple statements that were easily explained and backed up. Now, she thought, she was ready to start writing.

---

### Grant Seeking Tip

Whether you are required to write a letter of inquiry or an intent-to-apply letter, do everything necessary to ensure that your organization, program, or project fits the priorities of the foundation.

---

# Chapter 17

## The Initial Query

By the time you get to the point of writing your initial query or an intent-to-apply letter, you may have spoken with someone at the foundation on the phone, exchanged a few e-mails, or perused the foundation Web site. The letter of inquiry or intent-to-apply letter, however, should be viewed as the first contact.

As we have been reading about Amicitia Community Gardens' plan, we have seen that Rose needed to write two letters that were to be mailed, and she would also file an electronic intent-to-apply over a foundation's Web site. No matter what the initial approach may be, what was most important was how the seeker frames the introduction. Rose had decided that she needed to take a slightly different approach with each of the letters she would be writing.

Rose felt the most confident about the intent-to-apply letter she would write to the Westview Community Foundation because she spoke with someone who was familiar with Amicitia Community Gardens and knew a member of her board of directors. She decided that this would be the first letter she would write.

The letter of inquiry to the XYZ Foundation would be the second letter she would write because she felt like she understood the funding priorities of this foundation the most. She also felt that she had a good handle on how to match her organizational needs to those priorities.

To write the intent-to-apply letter to the Herald Foundation, Rose felt that she needed to understand the technological needs of her organization a little better. To do this, she needed to sit down with the person who handled Amicitia Community Gardens' Web site. This would be the third letter she would write.

At this point, you might be wondering what the difference is between a letter of inquiry and an intent-to-apply letter. They accomplish the same task; however, there are some minor differences:

- **The letter of inquiry** is required by organizations that are new faces to funders. The inquiry is made just to ensure that the applying organizations understand the funding priorities of the funder.

- **Intent-to-apply letters** are submitted by organizations that have received past funding from the funder and have an understanding as to the purpose and priorities of the funding foundation. Often, the terms are used interchangeably. Notice Rose's directive to submit an intent-to-apply letter to the Herald Foundation, a foundation she has not received past funding from. Rose was asked to submit an intent-to-apply letter to the Westview Community Foundation because a board member had a contact at the Foundation, so there was an existing relationship. You will begin to note the importance of relationship building as we proceed in this process.

Rose settled in to write an intent-to-apply letter to the Westview Community Foundation. Rose had learned in her research that these types of letters should be one to three pages long. She knew she had to spell out her case, but she did not need to go into the details of the project. If the foundation accepted her initial proposition, an application process would follow allowing her to define the fundamentals of the project. She first considered what should go into the letter.

**An intent-to-apply letter should include:**

- An introductory statement of proposition, amount of request, and program duration

- A statement of need that simply defines why the project is necessary and what the organization is currently doing in respect to the defined need

- A description of the organization

- A description of the proposed project

- A budgetary impact statement

- A closing restatement of request

# Sample Intent-to-Apply Letter

*Amicitia Community Gardens*
*1530 Burr Oak Drive*
*Westview, IN 46323*
*Rose Flowers, Executive Director*

*Robert Town*
*Executive Director*
*Westview Community Foundation*
*P.O. Box 789*
*Westview, IN 46322*

*Dear Mr. Town:*

*Thank you for taking the time to speak with me last week. Also, thank you for the invitation to submit this intent-to-apply letter to the Westview Community Foundation. Amicitia Community Gardens intends to submit a proposal to the Westview Community Foundation to fulfill its organizational capacity-building objective of having a community garden in every precinct of the city within the next three years. To achieve this objective, Amicitia Community Gardens requests a grant of $20,000 a year over the next three years. This letter of intent is being submitted as per the Westview Community Foundation's invitation to Amicitia Community Gardens.*

*Amicitia Community Gardens is a community gardening cooperative whose mission is to assist families, neighborhoods, and organizations in growing food for themselves and the community. Amicitia Community Gardens is a friendly organization where all community members can come together to cultivate our connection to nature and each other by growing food locally. Amicitia Community Gardens envisions an environmentally educated community in which people of all ages and backgrounds are encouraged to learn how to garden, re-connect with the land, and connect with our community.*

*Amicitia Community Gardens, a name which translates to "friendship," was first established by a group of strong-minded, committed Westview neighbor-hood residents who took part in a citywide program offered by the Nature Conservancy in 2001 to create green spaces in urban neighborhoods around the* country. The first Amicitia Community Garden was planted in a 70- by 70-foot vacant lot in the Westview neighborhood, a residential neighborhood that, at the time, appeared to be in poor condition. Much of the neighborhood was made up of large apartment buildings with very few single-family homes. The lot that Amicitia Community Gardens' first garden was planted on had been a vacant lot for nearly 20 years.

As many of the residents of the Westview neighborhood are immigrant families, many of them have come from places where gardening and farming was an important way of life. Thus, the desire of the neighborhood residents to develop a community garden took root with a dynamic cause. The community was committed to stopping the appearance of tarnish and establishing a little bit of "home" in this new land.

Amicitia Community Gardens' first garden was planted in the spring of 2001. At this time, 12 families took part in the garden's development. In that first year, the gardeners grew tomatoes, peppers, bok choy (an Asian vegetable in the cabbage family), carrots, cabbage, and several kinds of beans. Flowers were also grown around the garden's periphery. Those that planted it enjoyed the garden's produce; the entire neighborhood enjoyed the flowers. Sixteen families planted the garden the following year, and we were running short on space for new gardeners to plant as more and more people were interested in Amicitia Community Gardens. Local television coverage of the garden in full summer ripeness made the entire city aware of our program in that second year.

In April of 2003, several of the gardeners were asked to visit classrooms in schools around the city to talk about neighborhood gardens. The children in several schools started plants inside their classrooms and, as the weather grew warmer, those plants were moved out into the schoolyards. Gardening activities were offered during the summer months, with assistance from our neighborhood gardeners, in order to maintain the school gardens throughout the summer and to further the children's knowledge of gardening.

The next two summers saw an explosion of the neighborhood gardening movement in the city, with Amicitia Community Gardens at the forefront of this wonderful growth. Six more urban lots in four different city neighborhoods became community gardens, and Amicitia Community Gardens' mission changed from that of a singular community garden to an organization whose mission is to provide places where all community members can come together to cultivate our connection to nature and each other by growing food locally.

The capacity building project that Amicitia Community Gardens is proposing to the Westview Community Foundation falls in line with a primary objective of Amicitia Community Gardens' long-term strategic plan. A primary organizational goal is to develop the Community Garden Initiative. Toward that goal, and the project we are proposing to the Westview Community Foundation, we intend to have at least one community garden in each precinct of the city within the next three years.

The fulfillment of this Community Gardening Initiative will call on Amicitia Community Gardens to establish nine community gardens in nine precincts of the city over the next three years. To accomplish this objective, Amicitia Community Gardens must secure land on which to establish the gardens, make tools and sundry gardening necessities — such as seed, soil, and fertilizer — available to gardeners, recruit and train volunteer gardeners, and hire and train gardening associates.

Amicitia Community Gardens plans to have two new gardens in place by next spring, three more gardens planted in the following spring, and the final four gardens in the project planted the third spring. We have begun communicating with the City of Westview about locating desirable locations for the first two gardens in this project, though no locations have yet been identified.

Amicitia Community Gardens' request for $60,000 over a three-year period from the Westview Community Foundation will cover, for the most part, property acquisition. Amicitia Community Gardens has an excellent working relationship with the City of Westview and has been fortunate that the city places a high value on the work that Amicitia Community Gardens is doing. Funds from this capacity-building grant will also help to cover the costs of tools and sundry gardening necessities. Other costs associated with this project are covered in other grant proposals that are currently being written.

As Amicitia Community Gardens grows and moves toward its tenth year, its commitment to community gardening and community growth bloom right along with it. Amicitia Community Gardens has begun establishing relationships with citywide food banks to which our organization will provide fresh produce throughout the growing season, as well as fall/winter vegetables such as potatoes, sweet potatoes, and squash that will last into the winter. A similar relationship has been developed with a number of upscale restaurants to provide fresh, locally grown herbs and vegetables during the summer months. Charitable and business opportunities abound for our neighborhood gardeners. A farmers' market has been established next to our first Westview neighborhood community garden to sell produce and flowers and to spread the word about our program.

We are confident that the Community Gardening Initiative will help grow the capacity of Amicitia Community Gardens and will help it to achieve its mission-driven goals over the next three years. We thank the Westview Community Foundation for the invitation to make this proposal. We look forward to partnering with you to help make Westview a green place to live.

*Respectfully,*
*Rose Flowers*
*Executive Director*
*Amicitia Community Gardens*
*1530 Burr Oak Drive*
*Westview, IN 46323*

Rose has written a good intent-to-apply letter. She makes her case and clearly describes the project that Amicitia Community Gardens will propose for funding. She states the mission of the organization, expresses the organization's needs clearly, speaks to the amount of funding and what it will be used for, and puts it all into a definite schedule.

However, keep in mind that there is no such thing as the perfect letter-of-intent or perfect query letter. Rose has done a good job, though, for her first letter of this type. Some people assume that the perfect letter is the one that always gets positive results, but that is not possible. You will be rejected from time to time, no matter how good your letter may be. The best thing that Rose had going for her in this case was that she had received an invitation to apply, so the foundation was already aware of her organization and the positive work it was doing in the community. That is a good place to start.

There are sections of Rose's letter that you probably recognized, such as the mission and vision stated in the section of the letter that she used to define her organization. There is no better way to define your organization than to state your mission. You likely also recognized the history of the organization was also included, which she used as her needs statement. Amicitia Community Gardens was born out of a community need to stop urban tarnish; their solution was the community garden.

The best thing about Rose's letter is that it is sincere and shows a conviction to the organizational mission. Even though Rose knew she had certain points to make in writing this intent-to apply letter, her letter does not come off as formulaic. Her letter is businesslike, but it carries with it the heart and soul of Amicitia Community Gardens.

Rose ran her letter by another member of her staff, who reviewed it for grammar and spelling errors and for factual discrepancies. The letter was deemed excellent. Rose then took it to the individual on her board of directors who recommended her to the Westview Community Foundation. The board member thought that Rose's letter made the case well and believed that the foundation would ask her to submit a full proposal.

Rose mailed her intent-to-apply letter to the Westview Community Foundation and made a note on her calendar to call them in a couple of days to confirm their receipt. She then proceeded to work on her second letter: the letter of inquiry to the XYZ Foundation.

The letter of inquiry to the XYZ Foundation would address many of the same points from the letter of intent to the Westview Community Foundation, but this letter had something of a different task to fulfill. Rose was about to write a letter to a foundation that knew nothing of Amicitia Community Gardens — this letter would act as an introduction.

You will note much of the same information from the intent-to-apply letter is in the letter of inquiry. However, this letter involves a different project, and Rose did not have an acquaintance at this foundation as she had with the Westview Community Foundation.

## Grant Seeking Tip

In the same manner that you sought to assure that your needs matched the foundation's priorities, make sure that you do what you can to determine the best way to approach a foundation. Some foundations ask that you write a letter, while others suggest you call.

### A Letter of Inquiry should include:

- An introductory statement
- A statement explaining how you found their foundation
- A description of how your proposed project relates to the foundation
- A description of the organization
- A short description of the proposed project
- A closing statement containing information about how you will contact them next

## Sample Letter of Inquiry

*Rose Flowers, Executive Director*
*Amicitia Community Gardens*
*1530 Burr Oak Drive*
*Westview, IN 46323*

*XYZ Charitable Foundation*
*Mr. Samuel Zander Jr., President*
*Box 432*
*Blanton, IN 44444*

*Dear Mr. Zander:*

*Due to the XYZ Foundation's interest in agriculture, horticulture, and education, Amicitia Community Gardens would like to inquire about submitting a proposal for funding. We are confident that the mission and vision of Amicitia Community Gardens clearly matches the priorities of the XYZ Foundation.*

*Amicitia Community Gardens would like to submit a proposal to the XYZ Foundation for $45,000 that would help us to hire and train nine part-time gardening associates over the next three years, beginning next fiscal year. As our organization is poised to take a great leap forward in terms of the number of gardens we help tend, gardening associates are valuable team members as we work in more neighborhoods within our community. Gardening associates work in our community gardens and in local schools as teachers and local experts in organic gardening. In the community gardens, the associates are the professionals who help the neighborhood gardeners learn and understand the art of growing fruits, vegetables, and flowers. In the schools, the associates work with children on a variety of projects such as schoolyard gardens and classroom greenhouses.*

*In light of your support of community gardens and other agricultural and educational initiatives in the region, we feel that you might like to partner with Amicitia Community Gardens in our mission to continue planting community gardens in the city. We would very much like to speak with you about your application process and the possibility of a partnership.*

*Amicitia Community Gardens, incorporated in the State of Indiana, is a federally recognized 501(c)(3) charitable organization. Amicitia Community Gardens is a community gardening cooperative whose mission is to assist families, neighborhoods, and organizations in growing food for themselves and the community. Amicitia Community Gardens is a friendly organization where all community members can come together to cultivate our connection to nature and each other by growing food locally. Amicitia Community Gardens envisions an environmentally educated community in which people of all ages and backgrounds are encouraged to learn how to garden, reconnect with the land, and connect with our community.*

*I will call you next week to talk further about Amicitia Community Gardens. I thank you for your consideration, and I look forward to speaking with you.*

*Respectfully,*
*Rose Flowers*

Rose has accomplished a number of things in her letter of inquiry to the XYZ Foundation. She has, it seems, covered the basics of what was required in the foundation guidelines that Rose had read. The guidelines stated, "Organizations considering submitting proposals to the XYZ Foundation should make inquiries about our priorities, the application process, and the funding schedule well before the beginning of the project." By following these guidelines, Rose showed the foundation that she had researched their foundation. She also stated that she knew from their Web site that their priorities included agriculture and education. These are good points to make because they show your dedication and will impress the foundation.

She stated that the project Amicitia Community Gardens was considering would begin in their next fiscal year. This, she hoped, was well enough in advance for them to consider. Rose ended the letter stating that she would follow-up with a call to talk about the grant application process.

Along with the information that the foundation asked for in an inquiry, Rose introduced her organization by stating the organizational mission. She spoke a little bit about the project that Amicitia Community Gardens would like to propose to the foundation, and she let them know that Amicitia Community Gardens is a recognized not-for-profit corporation. She matched the foundation priorities to the project in this letter.

Rose felt that she could omit a needs statement for now. While there is a need for gardening associates stated in the letter, she thought that a full needs statement was something to included in a full proposal. Some foundations may ask for a statement of need in an inquiry, but the XYZ Foundation did not.

As we have now seen in both of the letters that Rose has written, she was well-prepared with all the information requested because she did her research. All of her attention to details like organizational mission and vision, strategic planning, and history — as well as her work with her stakeholders — proved to be well-worth her time.

Again, Rose ran her letter of inquiry past a staff member and a member of her board of directors. Both individuals thought that she had done what was asked of her and was clear and concise in her inquiry.

Rose's third foray into her quest for foundation funding was to be submitted via a corporate foundation's Web site. Rose had decided to approach the Herald Foundation to assist Amicitia Community Gardens in expanding their Web site and communications abilities. Rose created an account at the Herald Corporation site and navigated to the Herald Foundation. There, she found a link titled "Intent-to-Apply."

## Sample Online Intent-to-Apply

An online intent-to-apply letter is one that will be submitted through a foundation's Web site, formatted like many online applications. There will be specific fields to enter and directions to follow. You will know if your foundation wants you to submit an intent-to-apply letter online by consulting their guidelines. These applications can be pages long, but they will require most of the same information in the intent-to-apply letter shown earlier.

Rose went to the foundation's Web site to complete the online intent-to-apply form. The first page of the intent-to-apply form consisted of fields in which Rose could fill out contact information, declare that Amicitia Community Gardens was a 501(c) (3), and inform the foundation what kind of assistance Amicitia Community Gardens was seeking. In this last field, there were many options to choose from; Rose checked *Technology Grant.*

The second page of the form asked for the purpose of your organization. In this field, Rose typed the organizational mission and vision statement.

The third page of the form asked for a brief description of the proposed project. Rose wrote:

*The goal is to expand and strengthen the organization's existing communications tools by increasing our Web capabilities and increasing the size and scope of the organizational newsletter. Making these improvements in our communications tools will facilitate exchange of ideas and information among families, educators, and gardeners involved in Amicitia Community Gardens programs. The improved Web site will also provide a space for the online seed sales initiative. The expanded newsletter will offer many of the same improvements that the Web site offers to people who are without access to computers.*

The fourth page of the form asked Rose to briefly describe the need for this project. Rose wrote:

*Amicitia Community Gardens has experienced dramatic growth over its first ten years of existence. Within the next three years, it is our plan to have a community garden in every precinct of the city, have a presence in many of Westview's public schools, have classes in organic gardening in the city's community colleges, and have a major backyard garden initiative. From our growth in the first ten years and our projected growth over the next three years, we see that community gardening fills a need within our urban environment. Linking all of our stakeholders together via a strong Web presence and with an informational tool like a newsletter is vital to keeping our mission and vision strong and clear.*

The fifth and final page of the form asked to briefly specify the funding requirements. In this field, Rose simply typed $15,000. The final questions asked about the time frame of the project. Rose typed that funding would be needed in the next fiscal year.

---

## Grant Seeking Tip

Before signing on to fill out any online grant information, take some time to peruse the form first. You will present a more effective application if you make note of the questions asked, compose your answers in a separate document, and cut and paste your information into the desired field. Read the entire application before you begin to fill it out.

---

Rose hit the submit button and received a confirmation e-mail that stated that she would be notified if the Herald Foundation wished for submission of a full proposal.

The online submission seems successful. The foundation requested specific information, and Rose was specific and brief in her replies. Having done her early research, she knew what she wanted and with this, her third letter-of-intent/inquiry in as many weeks, she had developed a clear, concise way of framing her answers.

As we look back on all of Amicitia Community Gardens' letters, the two words "clear" and "concise" cannot be stressed enough.

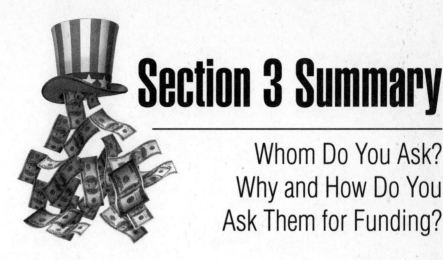

# Section 3 Summary

## Whom Do You Ask?
## Why and How Do You
## Ask Them for Funding?

Here you have identified the foundations that you will make proposals to and have made your initial contact. You have seen how important your early work was in terms of putting together a mission and vision statement that is clear and concise — these steps are fundamental to the grant seeking process.

In our examples of letters written by Rose, we looked at three different ways to make initial contact with foundations. However, there are many more ways that organizations introduce themselves to potential funders. The main point here is that when you are ready to make contact, be prepared to put your best foot forward. You are prepared when you have all the facts about your organization at your fingertips; you know where it is you are going; and you have a good idea as to how you want to get there.

# Part 1 Summary

As you have been reading and working your way through this guide, you could have been researching, collecting data, and writing along with our Amicitia Community Gardens Executive Director, Rose. If you have been following along, then you may have sent out some letters of intent and/or queries and are all set to write your grant(s).

The fundamentals of the grant writing process are things that should be practiced and kept up-to-date. Keeping these documents up-to-date will help make your life of grant writing easier.

## Grant $eeking Tip — The Fundamentals

- Have a clear, concise mission statement
- Have a clear vision statement
- Stay true to your mission and vision
- Make sure your goals are aligned with your mission
- Make sure your objectives and activities are SMART

A few more points to remember:

- Your strategic plan is an essential document. Keep it up-to-date. Refer to it often, and make changes as needed. Follow the plan and keep your goals in mind.

- Constantly update your organizational history. Knowing where you have been is as important as knowing where you are going.

- Assess your activities. Always ask why things are a success or why things fail. Assessment helps you learn from all your activities.

- Talk to your stakeholders. They are your most valuable assets. Listen to your stakeholders' suggestions and consider them when you are making proposals.

- Always work to bring your stakeholders closer to the center of your circle — they are your most valuable assets.

- Always look for new funding opportunities. The research you did exploring for foundations is an ongoing task. Read, talk, listen, and take note. You never know where the next opportunity will present itself.

- Know what you are asking for. Make it a simple statement, and keep the wordiness to a minimum. The simpler you frame your request, the better.

- Remember, you are looking for partnerships, not handouts.

# PART TWO

Writing The Proposal(s)

This part of the book will review the process of actually writing a grant proposal. The chapters will include numerous examples of proposal formats, cover letters, grant proposals, attachments, and thank-you letters.

There are a variety of basic formats in which foundations may ask for your grant to be submitted. Just as Rose was required to submit an online letter to a foundation's Web site, it is probable that when the time comes for writing the grant to that foundation, it will also be done online.

You will be asked to fill out a grant application form or prepare a narrative that will address a number of points required by the foundation. Some foundations ask for a combination of the two, as they provide an application form and ask for a narrative.

The grant application form may be an online form that you fill out directly on the foundation Web site, and you may download the form from the Web site and mail it back, or upload the completed form electronically to their site. Grant application forms vary from foundation to foundation. Some forms provide you with a given amount of space in which to provide your information, and you are asked to not exceed the given space; Some forms allow you to add additional pages if need be.

Many groups of grant makers, especially grant makers that share a common region, have adopted what is referred to as a "common grant application." This is a single proposal format that is shared by a specific community of funders to simplify the process, saving time — and money. If you come across a foundation that uses a common grant form, it is important to remember that every foundation has different guidelines, priorities, deadlines, and schedules. It is vital that you contact the foundation to inquire about their guidelines before you submit a common grant form to a potential funder. Any funder that has agreed to accept this form may request additional information as needed.

You may be asked to write proposals that are extended versions of the intent-to-apply letters. In other words, there will not be an application form, but you will write a narrative that will address specific issues that the foundation requests you address further.

Whether you fill out an online application, a common grant form, or write an extended narrative, it is crucial that you follow the exact directions set forth by the foundation. Many foundations will immediately discard any proposal that omits information, does not include all attachments, or is late in submitting, even if it is a minor omission.

Budgeting is a major factor in the grant writing process. In this chapter, there will be several budget examples. When applying for a grant, you will be required to submit a few different budgets when you submit your grant proposals. Foundations may ask to see:

- An annual budget that reflects your expenses and income for the current fiscal year
- Budgets for the fiscal year prior to the current year
- The current fiscal year's balance sheet
- A budget estimate for the next fiscal year
- A budget for the program you are proposing

You may be asked to provide an estimated budget with an intent-to-apply. If this is the case, the budget you supply can be a simplified budget. It should give enough information for the organization to determine the financial status of the organization, but it does have to be as detailed as a budget submitted with the proposal. We will talk more about budgets in this portion of the book. It is important that you start thinking about this matter as a part of your preparation process.

Now you are ready to start writing. Again, if you are seriously considering writing grant proposals, you should work right along with the book as we explore the grant writing process.

# Section 4

## The Grant Proposal(s)

We will continue to work with our fictional character, Rose Flowers, the Executive Director of Amicitia Community Gardens, as she writes her three grant proposals. She had received the approval of all three foundations she wrote letters to and is now ready to get down to the business of writing her grant proposals. We will examine each aspect of Rose's three grant proposals.

Rose will be required to submit grant proposals in three different formats. The Westview Community Foundation has sent her an application form along with the Foundation Guidelines. She will fill the form out and mail or hand-deliver it. The XYZ Foundation will require her to compose a narrative that addresses various issues pertaining to their guidelines. The Herald Foundation has an online application format that will require Rose to describe her project in a most succinct manner. Follow along with Rose and see the three ways that you may be required to submit your grant proposal.

# Chapter 18

## Proposal Contents

Every grant proposal you write will require you to follow specific grant guidelines. You can find the guidelines for the XYZ Foundation in Chapter 13; the guidelines for the Westview Community Foundation and the Herald Charitable Foundation follow in this chapter.

Let us look at the guidelines that Rose was sent when she received approval for a proposal from the Westview Community Foundation.

## Sample Grant Guidelines

The guidelines began with this letter to Amicitia Community Gardens:

*Dear Ms. Flowers and Amicitia Community Gardens:*

*At Westview Community Foundation, we believe communities that work together create the kinds of communities that are worth living and raising our children in. Through our grant-making programs, we support nonprofit orga-*

*nizations and community institutions that are improving our community in many different ways.*

*We view philanthropy as a process that brings together monetary support with organizations, institutions, and individuals that are committed to continuously making our community a better place for all who live here. Westview Community Foundation's Guidelines for Grant Proposals is our invitation to you to work with us in building a better and more vibrant community. While the Foundation most often makes grants to nonprofit organizations, we also consider grants to schools, churches, government agencies, and other funders working on projects that share our vision and are consistent with priorities within our program areas.*

*You have received this invitation to apply for funding from the Westview Community Foundation because your letter of intent was found to be consistent with our established priority of creating green space in our urban environment. This invitation to apply for a capacity-building grant is being offered to you in light of your work in creating community green spaces. Attached to this letter, you will find grant application guidelines that correspond to this specific program. You will also find instructions on applying for your grant and descriptions of the application process. Please follow this process and include all requirements so that the Foundation may have all the information needed to view your proposal.*

*Thank you for your interest in Westview Community Foundation. The Foundation is grateful to work with an organization that has the same values as the Foundation, and that shares our passion for building community together.*

*We look forward to receiving your proposal.*

*The Board of Directors of the Westview Community Foundation*

## *Westview Community Foundation Guidelines*

*You are invited to apply for a capacity-building grant to assist you in support of your community's efforts to revitalize your city by making green space available for gardeners, students, families, and the community-at-large. The Westview Community Foundation supports organizations that work to unite and strengthen a community. Citizens working to enhance, beautify, and/or better utilize common space projects, such as vacant lots, parks, and curb strips, are successful in achieving that goal. These kinds of projects also have a dramatic visual impact and result in greater change in a neighborhood and the city as a whole. Capacity-building projects that work to ensure the health, growth, and long-term vitality of organizations that are involved in developing urban green spaces are a priority to the Westview Community Foundation.*

## Application Process

1. Grant support is offered to neighborhood-based groups, community organizations, and youth organizations. Individuals are not eligible for support.

2. All groups are encouraged to talk with a representative of the Westview Community Foundation before considering an application.

3. Submit a completed application plus four copies of the completed application. All required materials (photos, letters of support, etc.) should only be attached to the original application.

4. All applications to the Westview Community Foundation Capacity-Building Program will be subject to a review process. The Westview Community Foundation staff will analyze each application for completeness and eligibility. Once this process is complete, they

will submit the applications to the board of directors for review and final decisions on funding.

5. Applicants chosen to receive funding will be notified by mail.

Included in the packet Rose received from the Westview Community Foundation was a two-page document that highlighted how Rose's funding proposal should be organized, and it enumerated a series of prompts that needed to be addressed. Rose addressed each of these prompts with the appropriate information.

The prompt from the foundation is in italics.

## Sample Grant Application Narrative

### 1. Describe your organization or group.

*Amicitia Community Gardens (ACG) is a community gardening cooperative whose mission is to assist families, neighborhoods, and organizations in growing food for themselves and the community. Amicitia Community Gardens is a friendly organization where all community members can come together to cultivate our connection to nature and each other by growing food locally. Amicitia Community Gardens envisions an environmentally educated community in which people of all ages and backgrounds are encouraged to learn how to garden, reconnect with the land, and connect with our community.*

*ACG carries out this mission through four program areas: Family Garden Initiative, Neighborhood Garden Plots, Gardeners Mean Business, and Learning to Grow. Each of these program areas are tied directly to the mission of ACG.*

*A professional staff manages ACG. The staff, at the time of this plan, is made up of four full-time and six part-time employees. The full-time staff consists of an executive director, an office manager, a gardens manager, and an education director. The part-time staff consists of three gardening associates, a farmers' market manager, an education associate, and a landscape associate.*

*The stakeholders consist of our community of gardeners, volunteers, students, ACG Board of Directors, ACG staff, ACG sponsors, ACG funders, collaborative businesses and agencies, and the community-at-large.*

## Answer ) Analysis:

Rose knows that the best way to describe Amicitia Community Gardens is to state the mission and vision. She dove a little deeper into the organizational description by defining how the mission is carried out and who is involved in that process. She was able to define Amicitia Community Gardens beyond the mission and vision because she had the space to do so, and she was correct in feeling that the extended definition helped her cause. She would have been OK with only the mission and vision, though, if the space did not allow her to go further.

**2. Briefly describe your proposed capacity-building project. Be sure to make note of the time frame in which this project will take place.**

*The capacity building project that Amicitia Community Gardens is proposing to the Westview Community Foundation falls in line with a primary objective of Amicitia Community Gardens' long-term strategic plan. A primary organizational goal is to further develop the Community Garden Initiative. Toward that goal, and the project we are proposing to the Westview Community Foundation, we intend to have at least one community garden in each precinct of the city within the next three years.*

*The fulfillment of this Community Gardening Initiative will call on Amicitia Community Gardens to establish nine community gardens in nine precincts of the city over the next three years. To accomplish this objective, Amicitia*

*Community Gardens must secure land on which to establish the gardens, make tools and sundry gardening necessities (such as seed, soil, and fertilizer) available for gardeners, recruit and train volunteer gardeners, and hire and train gardening associates.*

*Amicitia Community Gardens plans to have two new gardens in place by next spring, three more gardens planted in the following spring, and the final four gardens in the project planted the third spring. We have begun talks with the City of Westview about locating likely locations for the first two gardens in this project, though no locations have yet been identified.*

## Answer Analysis:

Rose found that her response was easy to frame. Note that the project described has been lifted directly from the Amicitia Community Gardens long-term strategic plan. Because the project is an objective from the plan, it has the SMART attributes that plan objectives should have. Thus, it is the kind of project that is easily assessed. This fits well with what the foundation is looking for.

### 3. Briefly describe how this project will affect your organization.

*Establishing community gardens is the central focus of Amicitia Community Gardens' long-term strategic plan and is directly tied to the mission of our organization. By establishing community gardens in every precinct of Westview, we are better able to clarify our organizational vision of an environmentally educated community in which people of all ages and backgrounds are encouraged to learn how to garden, reconnect with the land, and connect with our community. Also, having gardens throughout the city will help us to carry out and accomplish other goals established in our long-term plans. These goals include assisting families in growing food for themselves, expanding our organizational educational initiatives, and helping community gardeners to explore the commercial options of gardening.*

## Answer Analysis:

Rose was able to look to her long-term plan for her response. She replied that the project is directly taken from the plan that is linked to the organizational mission and vision. She states that in meeting the objective of the proposed project, Amicitia Community Gardens furthers its mission, clarifies its vision, and builds the capacity of the organization by increasing the number of gardens and organizational stakeholders.

## 4. Briefly describe how your project will affect your community

*Amicitia Community Gardens can look to its history to see proof that the establishment of community gardens has a positive impact on the community. We envision a future for Amicitia Community Gardens and our community that mirrors that positive past.*

*Amicitia, a word that loosely translates to "friendship," was first established by a group of strong-minded and committed Westview neighborhood residents who took part in a citywide program offered by the Nature Conservancy in 2001 to create green spaces in urban neighborhoods around the country. The first Amicitia Community Gardens community garden was planted in a 70- by 70-foot vacant lot in the Westview neighborhood, a residential neighborhood that, at the time, appeared to be in poor condition. Much of the neighborhood is made up of large apartment buildings with very few single-family homes. The lot that Amicitia Community Gardens' first garden was planted on had been a vacant lot for nearly 20 years.*

*As many of the residents of the Westview neighborhood are immigrant families, many of them have come from places where gardening and farming was an important way of life. Thus, the desire of the neighborhood residents to develop a community garden took root with a dynamic cause. The community was committed to stopping the unattractiveness of the community and establishing a little bit of "home" in this new land.*

*Amicitia Community Gardens' first garden was planted in the spring of 2001. At this time, 12 families took part in the garden's development. In that first year, the gardeners grew tomatoes, peppers, bok choy, carrots, cabbage, and several kinds of beans. Flowers were also grown around the garden's periphery. Those that planted it enjoyed the garden's produce, and the entire neighborhood enjoyed the flowers. Sixteen families planted the garden the following year, and space was suddenly at a premium, as more and more people were interested in Amicitia Community Gardens. Local television coverage of the garden in full summer ripeness made the entire city aware of our program in that second year. In April 2003, several of the gardeners were asked to visit classrooms in schools around the city to talk about neighborhood gardens. The children in several schools started plants inside their classrooms and, as the weather grew warmer, those plants were moved out into the schoolyards. Gardening activities were offered during the summer months with assistance by our neighborhood gardeners in order to maintain the school gardens throughout the summer and to further the children's knowledge of gardening.*

*The next two summers saw an explosion of the neighborhood gardening movement in the city, with Amicitia Community Gardens at the forefront of this wonderful growth. Six more urban lots in four different city neighborhoods became community gardens, and Amicitia Community Gardens' mission changed from that of a singular community garden to an organization whose mission is to provide places where all community members can come together to cultivate our connection to nature and each other by growing food locally.*

## Answer Analysis:

To answer this query, Rose can look to the history of her organization to describe how Amicitia Community Gardens' past activities have affected the community-at-large. To do this, she lifts the narrative straight from the organizational history she wrote some months before.

Answering the inquiry as to how the project will affect the community is similar to stating the need for the project. Earlier, Rose used Amicitia Community Gardens' organizational history to create a needs statement in her intent-to-apply letter to the Westview Community Foundation.

The Westview Community Foundation is a local funder that is well-aware of Amicitia Community Gardens' activities. This fact works in Rose's favor. Amicitia Community Gardens already has something of a relationship with the foundation, the foundation asked her organization to apply for this grant, and one of her board members has a connection at the foundation. So, as Rose addresses how Amicitia Community Gardens' proposed program will affect the community, she is confident that the foundation already believes in their plans. Nonetheless, Rose feels it is important that she be as clear as possible in each of her responses.

**5. Briefly describe how your organization will assess the outcomes of this project.**

*The objective of this capacity-building project is to establish nine community gardens over a three-year-period so as to have a community garden in each precinct of the city at the end of this proposed grant period. Assessment of this basic premise of this program would begin with determining whether this objective was met.*

*Whether or not the primary objective of the proposed project was met, the assessment process would probe deeper into the issue of whether the organization built capacity due to this partnership.*

*Assessment is a time to ask questions of the organization and its stakeholders. As we embark on a capacity-building project, we would ask questions and gather data directly related to the question of growth. We will look at the number of families we were able to assist because of our increased capacity. We will get feedback from the families. We will determine whether we brought new stakeholders into the organization because of the program, and we will determine what did and did not work with this program. We will explore — whether we determine that we were successful or not — what might be done better next time.*

*After we have gathered and analyzed the data, we will determine what actions to take based on the outcome of the program. The actions that are determined because of these outcomes will become part of a revitalized long-term plan.*

## Answer Analysis:

We continue to see how important the preparatory work that Rose did was as she is asked to describe how her organization would assess the outcomes of the proposed project. Rose did the work beforehand and was therefore prepared to state her plan of assessment.

It is not only the plan of assessment that answers how you will assess a particular project; the project is easily assessed because it has those SMART attributes. You could say that assessment is built into the project itself.

**6. Describe any partners that will be involved in the project with you.**

*Amicitia Community Gardens has a very good working relationship with the City of Westview and has been fortunate that the city places a high value on the work that Amicitia Community Gardens is doing. The city has been and continues to be a valuable partner as they work with us to identify locations in city neighborhoods that would be compatible with our activities. These locations not only include garden spots, but also locations for potential farmers' markets.*

*Amicitia Community Gardens has begun establishing relationships with citywide food banks to provide fresh produce throughout the growing sea-*

*son, as well as fall/winter vegetables such as potatoes, sweet potatoes, and squash that will last into the winter. Relationships have been made with a number of upscale restaurants to provide fresh, locally grown herbs and vegetables during the summer months. Charitable and business partnership opportunities abound for our neighborhood gardeners. A farmers' market has been established next to our first Westview neighborhood community garden to sell produce and flowers and to spread the word about our program.*

## Answer Analysis:

Technically speaking, Amicitia Community Gardens does not have a partner involved in the proposed project. There is not a formal partnership agreement made with any one organization to work with Amicitia Community Gardens in its quest to establish a community garden in every precinct of Westview. Rose, however, does not come right out and say this. The response to this query may be viewed as questionable.

Rose's response to the query about partners first refers to the city of Westview. She states that the city has worked closely with Amicitia Community Gardens, and she even refers to the city as a valuable partner. This, however, is not necessarily, what the foundation has in mind asking for the description. Rose also refers to some of Amicitia Community Gardens' other relationships that are not the kinds of partners that the foundation had in mind when it asked for descriptions.

The question we have to ask here is whether Rose made the right decision in the way she framed her response to the partnership query. Will it appear to the foundation that she was trying to pad her organizational résumé? Will it appear that she did not understand the question?

The answer to these questions may lead us back to the fact that Rose feels she is writing the proposal to a foundation that knows her organization. She knows that she could have stated that Amicitia Community Gardens does not have a partner in this project, but she feels that those that she pointed to in her response were important stakeholders — though not necessarily partners. She might have better explained that in her response, but she feels fortunate in the fact that the Westview Community Foundation knows her organization. She might have answered the query differently had she been composing this proposal to a foundation that has no knowledge of Amicitia Community Gardens. To be clear, Rose might have begun her response by stating that Amicitia Community Gardens would be entering into this project without any official partners.

**7. Briefly describe the support you are seeking from the Westview Community Foundation.**

*Amicitia Community Gardens requests a capacity-building grant of $60,000 over a three-year period ($20,000 a year for three years) from the Westview Community Foundation. Foundation support will mostly cover property acquisition. Funds from this capacity-building grant will also help to cover the costs of tools and sundry gardening necessities. Other costs associated with this project are covered in other grant proposals that are currently being written.*

## Answer Analysis:

Since she had spoken with a foundation representative, Rose knew exactly how to respond. She knew what she was asking for, and knew that the foundation knew what to expect. She had yet to develop the exact budget for the proposal, but she was certain of the project and of the need.

**8. Briefly describe any long-term funding strategies (if applicable) for sustaining this effort.**

*Amicitia Community Gardens has been working diligently to construct a many-tiered, dynamic development plan. We continuously work to expand our circle of stakeholders who work and act as volunteers, contributors, and spreaders of our mission. We, our organization and community gardeners, have begun several commercial ventures that will assist in supporting not only our gardeners, but our organization as well. Through our growing farmers' markets and our increasing relationships with restaurants in the city, we are seeing an increase in our earned income. Our growing reputation as a well-grounded community organization that is true to our mission and has a clear vision is generating a great deal of interest from the funding community. This interest is helping us to see growth in our unearned income.*

*Besides the financial support we see from individual donors and from charitable foundations such as the Westview Community Foundation, we have noted a large increase in in-kind support over the past three years. Home Supply Stores, Vantage Superstores, and Westview Home Improvement have all been valuable in-kind contributors to our community gardens.*

*We are confident that the capacity-building grant we are proposing to the Westview Community Foundation can only help to continue build a support network that will positively affect Amicitia Community Gardens' long-term growth.*

## Answer Analysis:

The final query of the narrative asks Rose to briefly describe any long-term funding strategies for sustaining the project. This was another area where Rose felt unprepared to answer. However, she did understand the necessity of establishing a many-tiered development plan, and this is what she expressed in her reply. She refers to Amicitia Community Gardens' growing ability to earn income, as well as the increasing grant opportunities that are becoming available to them. She also makes note of the in-kind contributions that the organization is realizing. This is important because some of the support that Amicitia Community Gardens is requesting from the Westview Community Foundation can be sustained in the long-term via the in-kind contributions Rose refers to.

Again, the Westview Community Foundation knows Amicitia Community Gardens. Because of this fact, Rose feels that they will have some knowledge of her organization's ability to support her proposed project for the long-term. She does feel it is important, however, to reply to this final query clearly and as completely as possible.

*Please include the following attachments with your grant proposal:*

*1. Finances*

- *Most recent financial statement from most recently completed year, audited if available, showing actual expenses. This information should include a balance sheet, a statement of activities (or statement of income and expenses), and functional expenses*
- *The organization's most recent IRS Form 990*
- *Organization budget for current year, including income and expenses*
- *Project Budget, including income and expenses*
- *Additional funders. List names of corporations and foundations from which you are requesting funds, with dollar amounts, indicating which sources are committed or pending*

*2. List of board members and their affiliations*

*3. Brief description of key staff, including qualifications relevant to the specific request*

*4. A copy of your current IRS determination letter indicating tax-exempt 501(c) (3) status.*

This is, in full, Rose's first grant proposal. We will examine the attachments that she was asked to provide with the proposal in the next chapter as we group all of the attachments from the three proposals together.

Rose wondered, at this point, whether she should include an executive summary or a cover letter with her application. These are two items that she had come across early in her grant writing research. Neither item was asked for in the proposal guidelines outlined by the Westview Community Foundation.

# Grant Seeking Tip

Always be sure to thoroughly read and understand the foundation's guidelines. If you have any questions about the guideline contents, do not be afraid to call and ask.

An executive summary is a one or two-page synopsis of the grant proposal's main points. If it is requested, an executive summary is submitted with your grant proposal to serve as a digested form of your grant proposal. Rose felt that the intent-to-apply letter she wrote served as a summary of the proposal she was about to submit. Indeed, if you compare the two documents, you will note that much of the copy is the same.

The cover letter is more of an introduction to your organization and your proposal. Your cover letter should not be used as a proposal summary, but should indicate the thought, care, and research that went into the attached funding request. You should always approach potential funders as potential partners. A cover letter is a good place to make that kind of connection.

Rose decided that she would attach a cover letter to her capacity-building grant proposal to the Westview Community Foundation. Like an executive summary, a cover letter is not always requested. Some foundation guidelines may request a cover letter. If the guidelines do not call for a cover letter, use your judgment as to whether to include one. Rose considered the points that she wanted to make and outlined the letter in the following manner:

- Amicitia Community Gardens' contact information
- Response to invitation to apply
- Title of proposed project
- Type of grant requested
- Amount of request
- Connection to foundation priorities
- Follow-up statement
- Signature

Here is the cover letter Rose wrote to accompany her grant proposal:

# Sample Cover Letter

*Amicitia Community Gardens*
*1530 Burr Oak Drive*
*Westview, IN 46323*
*Rose Flowers, Executive Director*

*Robert Town*
*Executive Director*
*Westview Community Foundation*
*P.O. Box 789*
*Westview, IN 46322*

*Dear Mr. Town:*

*Thank you for the invitation to Amicitia Community Gardens to apply for a capacity-building grant from the Westview Community Foundation. We are honored to submit the enclosed proposal for partnership to you.*

*The capacity-building project we are proposing is the continuation of Amicitia Community Gardens' Initiative. In this proposal, Amicitia Community Gardens requests a capacity-building grant of $60,000 ($20,000 annually for three years) to help us achieve an organizational objective of establishing a community garden in every precinct of Westview within the next three years.*

*We believe that our proposal matches the funding priorities of the Westview Community Foundation, as we endeavor to create green space in our urban environment. In doing so, we believe that we are working as a partner with you to make our community a better place to live.*

*Again, we thank you for this opportunity to share our vision, and we look forward to working with you in the very near future. We will be in contact with you to offer you a tour of our gardens.*

*Our Best Regards,*
*Rose Flowers*

## Letter Analysis:

Rose's cover letter is everything it should be. It is short and to the point. It covers everything that she intends it to cover — everything that she outlines. She lets the Westview Community Foundation know that she is well-prepared, as she understands what it is they asked of her and her organization. Also, she lets them know that she will be contacting them to invite them on a tour of their gardens. Because this is a local foundation, inviting the foundation to the gardens is smart; this action is seen as reaching out to the foundation to form that strong relationship.

With this final response, Rose completed her narrative to the Westview Community Foundation and was ready to submit it to her stakeholders. She thought it was important for a member of her staff to read through it for any correction, criticism, and comment. She also thought that it would be important that the board member who first referred her to the foundation have a look at her work.

Both stakeholders that read through Rose's narrative thought that she had done a good job in defining the organization, the project, needs, and the funding request. Rose got high marks for her first proposal and was ready to send it to the foundation once she put all the attachments together. After she included her attachments, there was one more thing she had to do before she delivered it: It is crucial to double check your proposals' content and compare it to the foundation's guidelines.

You will probably read in nearly every foundation guideline's brochure you see that incomplete proposals will not be considered. Do not omit anything without first clearing it with someone at the foundation. If the foundation asks for five copies of the narrative, three copies of the budget, and eight copies of your board of directors list, give them exactly what they ask for.

Rose ran her proposal by someone on her staff to proofread it. Everything counts, including spelling and neatness. If the foundation asks that you bind your proposal, bind it. If there is no mention of how to present your proposal, the best thing to do is make sure it is as neat as possible. We will cover the variety of ways you might submit your proposal in later chapters.

We will now move on to Rose's second proposal, made to the XYZ Foundation. We covered the guidelines of the XYZ Foundation in Chapter 13. As per the foundation guidelines, Rose wrote a letter of inquiry to the XYZ Foundation and asked to submit a proposal for $45,000 that would help Amicitia Community Gardens to hire and train nine part-time gardening associates.

In response to her letter of inquiry to the XYZ Foundation, Rose received this letter:

*Dear Ms. Flowers:*

*Thank you for your letter of inquiry to the XYZ Foundation. We look forward to hearing more about your proposed project. We invite you to submit a request for funding that should be postmarked no later than April 30th.*

*Your grant proposal should be formatted in the following manner:*

## Section 1: Cover Letter (one page)

*The cover letter should state the purpose of the grant proposal and briefly describe how the proposal correlates with the mission and priorities of the XYZ Foundation.*

## Section 2: Narrative

*Please include the following information in your narrative:*

1. **Need**: *Define proposed project for funding. It is necessary that a case is made for the proposed project that shows why it is needed and how it meets the needs of the organization. It must be clear as to how the project fits within the overall mission and vision of the applicant organization. It is vital that this statement of need is brief and clear.*

2. **Qualifications**: *Applicant must define organizational history and explain how the organization is qualified to undertake the proposed project. Applicant must present proof of organizational experience, expertise, and ability to manage proposed project.*

3. **Financial Ability**: *Applicant organization must present proof of financial stability, ability, and sound practice. Organization must present a view of the organizational budget in relation to the proposed project budget. Definition must also be given of overall organizational development plan, with particular emphasis placed on project sustainability after grant period. It is vital that this statement of financial ability is accurate.*

4. **Partnerships**: *Cooperative projects and ventures, when appropriate, will often strengthen an application. If a collaborative project is proposed, the role of each organization must be defined. The application must also define the benefit to each of the organizations in the partnership.*

5. **Assessment**: *Application must contain a defined assessment strategy that spells out the method to be employed to measure the effectiveness of the project following the grant period.*

6. **Capacity Building**: *Definition should be given as to how the proposed project will help the applicant organization grow. Simply proving that the organization will provide sustainability for the project is not enough.*

## Section 3: Attachments

### Financial Attachments

1. Organization budget
2. Proposed project budget
3. Year-end financial statements, audit, and Sources of Income Table
4. Current (year-to-date) financial statements
5. Major contributors
6. In-kind contributions

*Explanation of items in financial attachments, if applicable*

### Other Attachments

7. Board of directors list
8. Proof of IRS federal tax-exempt status, dated within the last five years
9. Key staff
10. Annual report, if available
11. Final report from most recent XYZ Foundation Grant (if applicable)

*We look forward to hearing from you and considering your proposal. We thank you for your interest in the XYZ Foundation.*

*Sincerely,*
*Mr. Samuel Zander, Jr., President*
*The XYZ Charitable Foundation*

As in her grant proposal to the Westview Community Foundation, Rose decided to write her cover letter after she wrote the narrative of her grant proposal, but for the sake of example, we will include the cover letter and narrative here in the order that Rose compiled them in her submission.

Before we look at Rose's grant proposal to the XYZ Foundation, it is important to remind you that it will be a little different from the proposal to the Westview Community Foundation in several ways.

As we have seen from the guidelines above, the format of the submission is different. Rather than answer a series of questions, Rose will compose an extensive narrative that will address the issues put forth in the guidelines.

The XYZ Foundation is not familiar with Amicitia Community Gardens beyond what they learned from the letter of inquiry that Rose sent. Thus, Rose's cover letter will need be more specific about her organization.

### *Sample Cover Letter*

*Amicitia Community Gardens*
*Rose Flowers, Executive Director*

*XYZ Charitable Foundation*
*Mr. Samuel Zander Jr., President*
*Box 432*
*Blanton, IN 44444*

Dear Mr. Zander:

Thank you for your invitation for Amicitia Community Gardens to apply for a grant from the XYZ Foundation. We are confident that the vitality of our mission, clarity of our vision, and purpose of our proposal are aligned with the priorities of the XYZ Foundation.

As the priorities of the XYZ Foundation include agriculture, horticulture, and education, Amicitia Community Gardens is submitting this proposal for $45,000 to help us hire and train nine part-time gardening associates over the next three years. The gardening associates serve our mission as Amicitia Community Gardens plans to greatly expand its operations over the next three years. Amicitia Community Gardens' operations are expanding in the neighborhoods, schools, and colleges of Westview. The need to assist and educate the family gardeners, community gardeners, and student gardeners has never been greater.

Amicitia Community Gardens has grown significantly over the first years of our existence. From a single community garden tended by a small handful of caring neighbors, to seven large gardens scattered throughout the city, Amicitia Community Gardens plans to have a community garden in every precinct of Westview within the next three years. We invite the XYZ Foundation to partner with us in the greening of the city.

We hope you enjoy reading our proposal. We look forward to working with you to help our city grow.

Rose Flowers
Executive Director
Amicitia Community Gardens

# Sample Grant Proposal

## Mission and Vision

Amicitia Community Gardens is a community gardening cooperative whose mission is to assist families, neighborhoods, and organizations in growing food for themselves and the community. Amicitia Community Gardens is a friendly organization where all community members can come together to cultivate our connection to nature and each other by growing food locally. Amicitia Community Gardens envisions an environmentally educated community in which people of all ages and backgrounds are encouraged to learn how to garden, reconnect with the land, and connect with our community. As Amicitia Community Gardens grows, we must also grow our ability to educate our community. As such, to fulfill our mission and realize our vision, we need to hire and train nine part-time gardening associates over the next three years, beginning next fiscal year. Gardening associates are valuable team members as we work in more and more neighborhoods within our community. Gardening associates work in our community gardens and in local schools as teachers and local experts in organic gardening. In the community gardens, the associates are the professionals that help the neighborhood gardeners to learn and understand the art of growing fruits, vegetables, and flowers. In the schools, the associates work with children on a variety of projects, such as schoolyard gardens and classroom greenhouses.

## History

Amicitia Community Gardens, a name that loosely translates to "friendship," was first established by a group of strong-minded and committed Westview neighborhood residents who took part in a citywide program offered by the Nature Conservancy in 2001 to create green spaces in urban neighborhoods around the country. The first Amicitia Community Gardens was planted in a 70- by 70-foot vacant lot in the Westview neighborhood, a residential neighborhood that, at the time, appeared to be in poor condition. Much of the neighborhood is made up of large apartment buildings with very few *single-family homes. The lot that Amicitia Community Gardens' first garden was planted on was a vacant lot for nearly 20 years.*

*As many of the residents of the Westview neighborhood are immigrant families, many of them have come from places where gardening and farming was an important way of life. Thus, the desire of the neighborhood residents to develop a community garden took root with a dynamic cause. The community was committed to establishing a little bit of "home" in this new land.*

*Amicitia Community Gardens' first garden was planted in the spring of 2001. At this time, 12 families took part in the garden's development. In that first year, the gardeners grew tomatoes, peppers, bok choy, carrots, cabbage, and several kinds of beans. Flowers were also grown around the garden's periphery. Those that planted it enjoyed the garden's produce; the entire neighborhood enjoyed the flowers. Sixteen families planted the garden the following year, and space was suddenly at a premium, as more and more people were interested in Amicitia Community Gardens. Local television coverage of the garden in full summer ripeness made the entire city aware of our program in that second year. In April 2003, several of the gardeners were asked to visit classrooms in schools around the city to talk about neighborhood gardens. The children in several schools started plants inside their classrooms and, as the weather grew warmer, those plants were moved out into the schoolyards. Gardening activities were offered during the summer months with assistance by our neighborhood gardeners in order to maintain the school gardens throughout the summer and to further the children's knowledge of gardening.*

*The next two summers saw an explosion of the neighborhood gardening movement in the city, with Amicitia Community Gardens at the forefront of this wonderful growth. Six more urban lots in four different city neighborhoods became community gardens, and Amicitia Community Gardens' mission changed from that of a singular community garden to an organization whose mission is to provide places where all community members can come together to cultivate our connection to nature and each other by growing food locally.*

## The Future Need

*As Amicitia Community Gardens grows and moves toward its tenth year, its commitment to community gardening and community growth bloom right along with it. Amicitia Community Gardens has begun establishing relationships with citywide food banks to provide fresh produce throughout the growing season, as well as fall/winter vegetables such as potatoes, sweet potatoes, and squash that will last into the winter. Relationships have been made with a number of upscale restaurants to provide fresh, locally grown herbs and vegetables during the summer months. Charitable and business opportunities abound for our neighborhood gardeners. A farmers' market has been established next to our first Westview neighborhood community garden to sell produce and flowers, and to spread the word about our program.*

*Amicitia Community Gardens has recently gone through a long-term strategic planning program and established a variety of goals and objectives to guide its growth over the next three to five years. A priority set forth in the plans developed by Amicitia Community Gardens and its closest stakeholders is the establishment of a community garden in every precinct of the Westview. This is a big step for our organization, but we are convinced that our history and the commitment of our stakeholders will make this endeavor successful.*

*The future looks bright for Amicitia Community Gardens and community gardening. We look forward to the sun and the rain. The first ten years has brought us a bountiful harvest, and we anticipate the cornucopia of the next ten seasons.*

*Amicitia Community Gardens' growth in terms of garden numbers and stakeholders has also resulted in financial growth and ability beyond our wildest dreams and expectations ten years ago. Each year's growth has brought with it an increased opportunity for further growth. The attached organizational and program budgets tell only a part of our financial story. The other parts of that story can be seen in our long-term strategic plan. Developmental initiatives in our plans call for increases in earned and unearned income. Successful farmer's market initiatives will be expanded, and successful seed stock initiatives will be expanded. The planned increase in garden numbers will result in a nearly 50-percent increase in gardener stakeholders over the next three years.*

## Partners

*Presently, our major partners are our stakeholders throughout the city. We have included in our long-term plans educational outreach initiatives in the city public schools and community colleges. We have begun outreach initiatives with the city food banks as well as a number of upscale restaurants. In addition, the City of Westview is a valuable partner in helping us grow our organization as they work closely with us to identify locations for our community gardens.*

## Objective and Assessment

*The objective of this proposed project is to hire and train nine associate gardeners over a three-year period. Assessment would begin with determining whether this objective was met.*

*Whether or not the primary objective of the proposed project was met, the assessment process would probe deeper into the issue of whether the organization built capacity because of this intended growth and whether the growth is sustainable.*

*Assessment is a time to ask questions of the organization and its stakeholders. As we embark on a capacity-building project, we would ask questions and gather data directly related to the question of growth. We will look at the number of families, students, and community gardeners we were able to assist because of our increased capacity. We will get feedback from those affected by our program. We will determine whether we brought new stakeholders into their organization because of the program, and we will determine what did and did not work with this program. We will explore whether we are successful and analyze what might be done better next time.*

*After we have gathered and analyzed the data, we will determine what actions to take based on the outcome of the program. The actions that are determined because of these outcomes will become part of a revitalized long-term plan.*

*The proposed project will help Amicitia Community Gardens grow as it achieves an important part of our organizational long-term strategic plan. That plan is directly tied to our mission. Our associate gardeners are educators as well as gardeners. Amicitia Community Gardens envisions an environmentally educated community in which people of all ages and backgrounds are encouraged to learn how to garden, reconnect with the land, and connect with our community.*

## Evaluation

To determine how successful Rose was in composing her narrative grant proposal, we need to go back to look at the proposal guidelines and see how well she addressed each point. Before we examine the narrative, let us look at the cover letter Rose wrote.

The question we need to ask is: Did Rose's cover letter do the job that she wanted it to do? Remember, the XYZ Foundation asked that a cover letter accompany the proposal and that the letter include the purpose of the grant request and a brief description of how the request fit with the mission and priorities of the XYZ Foundation. Rose also wanted to make sure that the cover letter served as a brief introduction to Amicitia Community Gardens. The difference between this proposal and the proposal she wrote to the Westview Community Foundation, if you recall, is that the XYZ Foundation had no prior knowledge of or experience with Amicitia Community Gardens.

Rose's cover letter has a few weaknesses, however. Rose was extremely focused on the mission and priorities of the XYZ Foundation. She tries to align the mission of Amicitia Community Gardens to those of the Foundation, but she misses the mark in her initial attempt. She misses because she explains that:

*As the priorities of the XYZ Foundation include agriculture, horticulture, and education, Amicitia Community Gardens is submitting this proposal for $45,000 to help us hire and train nine part-time gardening associates over the next three years. The gardening associates serve our mission as Amicitia Community Gardens Community Gardens plans to greatly expand its operations over the next three years. Amicitia Community Gardens' operations are expanding in the neighborhoods, schools, and colleges of Westview. The need to assist and educate the family gardeners, community gardeners, and student gardeners has never been greater.*

This explanation almost totally omits, or makes no mention of, Amicitia Community Gardens' mission. Yes, she states that the gardening associates serve the organizational mission, but she does not say what that mission is.

Here is the question: Does Rose need to state the mission of Amicitia Community Gardens in this cover letter? You have read that you should not state in the cover letter what you would be stating in the proposal. Does that apply here? It does not, because the guidelines asked for specific information to be stated in the cover letter. While the guidelines did not directly ask that Rose state the mission of her organization, they did ask her to state how the project aligned with the mission and priorities of the foundation. For Rose to state that the project aligns with the priorities of the foundation — and she does state those priorities — as well as the mission of Amicitia Community Gardens, she should state, in some manner, how the project relates to the mission of her organization. It should be clear. As it is currently stated, it is not clear.

Rose did run her proposals by a staff member. The person who read Rose's cover letter suggested a few minor changes to her letter, and this is what she came up with:

# Sample Cover Letter (Edited Version)

*Amicitia Community Gardens*
*Rose Flowers, Executive Director*

*XYZ Charitable Foundation*
*Mr. Samuel Zander Jr., President*
*Box 432*
*Blanton, IN 44444*

*Dear Mr. Zander:*

*Thank you for your invitation to Amicitia Community Gardens to apply for a grant from the XYZ Foundation. We are confident that the vitality of our mission, clarity of our vision, and purpose of our proposal are aligned with the priorities of the XYZ Foundation.*

*As the priorities of the XYZ Foundation include agriculture, horticulture, and education, Amicitia Community Gardens is submitting this proposal for $45,000 to help us hire and train nine part-time gardening associates over the next three years. Amicitia Community Gardens' mission is to assist families, neighborhoods, and organizations in growing food for themselves and the com-*

munity. *We envision an environmentally educated community in which people of all ages and backgrounds are encouraged to learn how to garden, reconnect with the land, and connect with our community. The gardening associates serve our mission, as Amicitia Community Gardens plans to expand its operations over the next three years. Amicitia Community Gardens' operations are expanding in the neighborhoods, schools, and colleges of Westview. The need to assist and educate the family gardeners, community gardeners, and student gardeners has never been greater.*

*Amicitia Community Gardens has grown significantly over the first years of our existence. From a single community garden tended by a small handful of caring neighbors to seven large gardens scattered throughout the city, Amicitia Community Gardens plans to have a community garden in every precinct of Westview within the next three years. We invite the XYZ Foundation to partner with us in the greening of the city.*

*We hope you enjoy reading our proposal. We look forward to working with you to help our city grow together.*

*Rose Flowers*
*Executive Director*
*Amicitia Community Gardens*

With the insertion and slight rewording of the Amicitia Community Gardens' mission and vision statement to fit the context of the letter, clarity has been given to this introduction to the organization. The lesson learned here is how important it is to have another set of eyes go over your work. No matter how many times you read what you have written, it is always good to have someone who has not been laboring over the words examine it for clarity, consistency, and any spelling or grammatical errors that you may have made. Everything is important.

Now that the cover letter has been looked over by a stakeholder and editor, we can analyze the body of Rose's narrative. The XYZ Foundation asked that six main points be addressed in the narrative.

The first point that needed to be addressed was the definition of the proposed project for funding. A case was to be made for the proposed project that showed why it is needed and how it meets the needs of the organization. It was important that it be clear as to how the project fits within the overall mission and vision of Amicitia Community Gardens, and it was stressed that the needs statement be brief and clear.

Rose's first needs statement accomplished all that it needed to accomplish. In the opening paragraph of the narrative, she states the mission and vision of the organization and goes on to state:

*As Amicitia Community Gardens grows, we must also grow our ability to educate our community. As such, to fulfill our mission and realize our vision, we need to hire and train nine part-time gardening associates over the next three years, beginning next fiscal year. Gardening associates are valuable team members as we work in more and more neighborhoods within our community. Gardening associates work in our community gardens and in local schools as teachers and local experts in organic gardening. In the community gardens, the associates are the professionals who help the neighborhood gardeners to learn and understand the art of growing fruits, vegetables, and flowers. In the schools, the associates work with children on a variety of projects, such as schoolyard gardens and classroom greenhouses.*

What Rose accomplishes above is not only linking her project to the mission and vision of Amicitia Community Gardens, but she also links it to the mission and priorities of the XYZ Foundation — a good start.

The second point that the foundation asked Amicitia Community Gardens to make in its funding proposal was to define its organizational history and explain how the organization is qualified to undertake the proposed project. It was also stated that the applicant must present proof of organizational experience, expertise, and ability to manage proposed project.

Here again, Rose employs the organizational history that she wrote as she did her preparatory work. The history works well in explaining how the organization is qualified to undertake the proposed project. The history also presents proof of experience, expertise, and ability to manage the proposed project. It also helps to continue to underline the need for the project. Rose then closes this section with an excellent introduction to the next point by highlighting Amicitia Community Gardens' long-term strategic plan. By doing this, she is telling the XYZ Foundation that Amicitia Community Gardens has defined objectives that support the overall mission and vision of the organization. This indicates that Amicitia Community Gardens is well-qualified to follow through on its plans for growth.

Point three that the XYZ Foundation asked for in its proposal guidelines was proof of financial stability, ability, and sound practice. They asked that organizations present a view of the organizational budget in relation to the proposed project budget. The foundation also asked that definition be given for the overall organizational development, with particular emphasis placed on project sustainability after grant period. They state that it is vital that this statement of financial ability be accurate.

Rose makes another misstep in this first draft of her proposal narrative. She refers to Amicitia Community Gardens' growth; she refers the foundation to the organizational budget and the project budget; and she discusses the organizational long-term strategic plan. The problem is that she does not present a view of the organizational budget in relation to the proposed project budget. She also makes a case for sustainability, but it is not clearly noted as such. She discusses these points with her co-worker who has read through the narrative, and this paragraph gets a re-write. Here is what they came up with:

*Amicitia Community Gardens' growth in terms of garden numbers and stakeholders has also resulted in financial growth and ability beyond our wildest dreams and expectations ten years ago. Each year's growth has brought with it an increased opportunity for further growth. Ten years ago, Amicitia Community Gardens utilized the services of one volunteer gardening associate who worked with the families of our one community garden. As the organization grew, that one volunteer became three part-time gardening associates who work with seven community gardens. Our long-term development plans envision 12 part-time gardening associates that work with 16 community gardens, Westview Public Schools, and the local community college.*

*The growth of our gardens has also resulted in our financial growth, as well in the growth of our development plans. The attached organizational and program budgets tell only a part of our financial story. The other parts of that story can be seen in our long-term strategic plan. Developmental initiatives in our plans call for increases in earned and unearned income. With this two-tiered plan of financial growth comes a planned sustainability of our increase in staffing as we take on nine part-time associate gardeners. Successful farmers' market initiatives will be expanded, and successful seed stock initiatives will be expanded. The planned increase in garden numbers will result in a nearly 50 percent increase in gardener stakeholders over the next three years. However, this is only possible if we are able to hire and train the number of part-time associate gardeners called for in our plans for long-term growth.*

The slight re-write in these paragraphs that relate to financial ability, along with the financial information that will be attached to the proposal, has Rose feeling that she has accomplished what the XYZ Foundation has requested in this segment of the narrative.

The fourth area that Rose was asked to cover in her narrative related to partnerships that strengthen the project. As in her proposal to the Westview Community Foundation, Rose could not state that Amicitia Community Gardens was entering into this project with a specific "partner." And as in her previous proposal, she identified organizations and entities that they work closely with that strengthen her organization, but was careful not to say that any of the institutions mentioned are partners in the specific project that is being proposed. Rose might make the relationships she mentioned in this paragraph stronger by closely aligning them to the project she is proposing, but she feels that the alignment has already been made in the rewritten paragraph that we have just examined, related to the organization's financial abilities.

The fifth point that Rose needed to cover in her narrative to the XYZ Foundation was a defined assessment strategy that spelled out the method employed to measure the effectiveness of the project following the grant period. Rose's narrative here was almost word-for-word the assessment strategy she defined in her proposal to the Westview Community Foundation. This is the strategy that was developed at the start of the organization, and it has worked quite well for them.

An important note about assessment here is that as you compose your proposal, you are asked to spell out a plan of assessment, and once the proposal becomes the project and that project occurs, you will be asked to submit a final report to the foundation. At this point, it is vital that your planned assessment become a definitive action. We will examine final reports later in this book.

The final point that Rose covered in her narrative related to how the proposed project would help the organization grow. The guidelines further stated that simply proving that the organization would provide sustainability for the project is not enough.

Rose's case for capacity building here, while short and to-the-point, was, perhaps, too short. Her co-worker thought that a little more definition should be added to this statement, and Rose worked to expand her final paragraph. Here is what she came up with:

*The proposed project will help Amicitia Community Gardens grow as it achieves an important part of our organizational long-term strategic plan. That plan is directly tied to our mission. Our associate gardeners are educators as well as gardeners. The addition of nine part-time associate gardeners to our ranks will help us as we expand our outreach to the neighborhoods and schools of our city. Fulfilling our mission and realizing our vision is the best way we can build capacity. Amicitia Community Gardens envisions environmentally educated communities in which people of all ages and backgrounds are encouraged to learn how to garden, reconnect with the land, and connect with our community.*

With this final paragraph, Rose felt that she had a solid narrative that hit all the points required by the foundation guidelines. She double-checked those guidelines against the narrative she had written, and her co-worker read and reread the narrative.

Before Rose compiled the final package for submittal to the XYZ Foundation, she shared her narrative with a board member for a fresh set of eyes. She showed the board member the guidelines as well as the narrative. The board member approved of the narrative, and Rose prepared the proposal for submission. She had quite a list of attachments that needed to go along with this narrative.

Rose and her co-worker double-checked her contents, and she celebrated this — the second of her three-proposal marathon — by immediately diving into proposal number three.

As you recall, Rose's third proposal was to be filed electronically to the Herald Foundation. The proposed project, as described in her letter-of-intent to the foundation, was to expand and strengthen the organization's existing communications tools by increasing its Web capabilities, and the size and scope of the organizational newsletter. Making these improvements in the organization's communications tools would facilitate exchange of ideas and information among families, educators, and gardeners involved in Amicitia Community Gardens programs. The improved Web site would also provide a space for the online seed sales initiative. The expanded newsletter would offer many of the same improvements that the Web site offered, but to people who are without access to computers.

Rose received notification from the Herald Foundation that Amicitia Community Gardens' proposed project fit within the guidelines of the foundation and that they would accept a full proposal that was to be submitted via their Web site. When Rose filed her letter-of-intent, she had created an account with the Herald Foundation, and she logged-in to see what she needed to prepare. Because she was unfamiliar with preparing an online grant application, she felt it was important that she examine the Web site to work out a strategy.

As she read the online application form, she printed out a blank application so she could fill it out by hand first. She decided that her best strategy would be to prepare the responses to the foundation requests before she attacked the online form.

Rose prepared to file her online grant application just as carefully as she had all of her preparatory work. She wrote several drafts of each narrative item requested and had her co-worker proof the materials she had printed out, as well as Rose's responses to each item included in the proposal. Rose e-mailed her responses to several stakeholders for their input.

After Rose was sure that she had done due diligence to the proposal, she was set to once again sign-on to the Web site of the Herald Foundation to submit her application. Notice the contact information areas toward the end of this sample are blank, as well as the areas that ask for places to be checked off. The contact information is specific to your organization and is left blank in this example. Pay close attention to the example narrative; this will give you a good idea on how to word your online proposal.

## Sample Online Grant Application

*The Herald Charitable Foundation*
**Grant Application**
**Non-Profit Organization Form**
*The Herald Charitable Foundation endeavors to respect the diversity in communities where the Herald Corporation and its subsidiaries operate. The Foundation's guidelines do not restrict applicants based on their religion, race, gender, religion, nationality, or disability.*

*The Herald Charitable Foundation grants are awarded in three categories, all of which reflect our funding priorities.*

## *Technology*

*Our Technology grant supports the efforts of organizations in communities where we live and work for the purpose of meeting that community's need for quality access to information through technological enhancements. These grants are intended to help organizations provide their members and the community-at-large with new and improved technology necessary for meeting the ever-changing need for access to information.*

### *Technology Grant Desired Outcomes*
*Projects awarded grant funding in this area must evidence the ability to produce at least one of the following outcomes:*

- *Increased effectiveness of existing technology and technical resources employed by the applicant to serve its mission and community*
- *Increased availability of up-to-date, reliable information*
- *Delivery of new and improved programs through technical means that anticipate and meet the constantly changing, technical needs of the organization, its stakeholders, and the community-at-large*

*Projects evidencing the ability to produce at least one of these desired outcomes are given preference:*

- *Increased access to information for under-served urban and rural persons*
- *Increased computer and information literacy skills among urban and rural youth*
- *Enhanced online presence of nonprofit organizations in communities where the Herald Corporation has a presence*

*Literacy*

*Our Literacy grant-making supports initiatives that encourage, promote, and develop adult and youth literacy programs. We fund programs that endeavor to help every member of a community be engaged in civic life through the ability to read and write.*

*Literacy Grant Desired Outcomes*

*Projects awarded grant funding in this area must evidence of the ability to produce at least one of the following outcomes:*

- *Increased literacy level of a segment of the community*
- *Enhanced intergenerational ties that foster educational achievement*
- *Increased community ability to use the resources and services of the public library*

*Projects evidencing the ability to produce at least one of these desired outcomes are given preference:*

- *Demonstrated improved attitudes on the value of school, public, academic, and special libraries*
- *Enhanced organizational ability to improve literacy education to community-at-large*
- *Enhanced ability to create before-and-after school programs that partner public schools and communities to provide academic and literacy support and safe, constructive enrichment activities for students*
- *Enhanced ability to strengthen community communication on issues vital to community renewal*

## Instructions

*1. Please fill out the application completely. If any part of this application is not completed, including the specified attachments in the requested format, your request for funding will not be considered.*

**Please read through the instructions and grant application completely prior to beginning the application process.**

**Please note that responses can be saved in place for 24 hours. After that time, the page will go blank. If you cannot plan to complete the application within 24 hours, you should wait until such a time when you may do so.**

**Please do not type "see attached" or change format of the application — all information must be included in this application in its current format.**

**<u>We do not accept handwritten or mailed applications. We only accept applications submitted through this electronic application process.</u>**

*2. After you complete the application, print out a copy for your records before you submit. At the end of the narrative section, you will be asked to attach all required attachments in PDF format.*

**Deadline Dates: January 1 and July 1**

**Required Attachments**

*Please check each circle at left, indicating that you have included all required documentation.*

- *A copy of the nonprofit organization's current Internal Revenue Service tax-exempt determination letter confirming section 501(c) (3) and 509(a)(1, 2, or 3) of the tax code.*

- If the name on the proposal differs from the name on the IRS determination letter, please provide an explanation of the difference; if the nonprofit organization operates under the auspices of another nonprofit, acting as a fiscal agent, please provide the following:

  a. Current IRS tax-exempt letter of the fiscal agent.
  b. A letter from the executive officer of the fiscal agent on the fiscal agent's letterhead, certifying their fiscal responsibility for the organization submitting the proposal. Include the following language:

     "I certify that this organization, as fiscal agent, takes reasonable steps to ensure that grant funds are not ultimately distributed to terrorist organizations and that staff, board, and other volunteers have no dealings whatsoever with known terrorists or terrorist organizations."

- A list of organization Board members and their business affiliations.

- Statement of assurance signed by an officer of your organization (e.g., CEO, President, Executive Director, COO, CFO, Comptroller, or Treasurer) stating that all statements included herein are true.

### Financial Information
- Most recent audited financial statement. This information should include a balance sheet, statement of activities (or statement of income and expenses), and functional expenses.

- Organization budget for current year, including income and expenses.

- Project budget, including income and expenses (if request is for project support).

## Contact Information

Date of Application _____

Organization IRS/Employer Identification
Number (EIN) _____

Name of Organization _____

Address _____

City _____

State _____

ZIP _____

Phone _____

Fax _____

Web site _____

Chief Operating Officer _____

Phone _____

E-mail _____

Person completing this report (if different
from Chief Officer) _____

Title _____

Phone _____

E-mail _____


Is your organization tax-exempt? Yes No

If no, are you a public agency/unit of government? Yes No


## Proposed Project Information
## (Please respond using only space provided)

Under IRS 501(c) (3) and 509(a) (1, 2 or 3)

**Name of Nonprofit Organization** __Amicitia Community Gardens__

**Project Title** _____Communications Technology Upgrade_____


## Project Dates

Start _____

End _____

**Provide a brief summary of the project.**

Our proposed project is designed to expand and strengthen the organization's existing communications tools by increasing our Web capabilities and increasing the size and scope of the organizational newsletter. Making these improvements in our communications tools will facilitate exchange of ideas and information among families, educators, and gardeners involved in Amicitia Community Gardens' programs. The improved Web site will also provide a space for the online seed sales initiative. The expanded newsletter will offer many of the same improvements that the Web site offers, but to people who are without access to computers.

**Provide a brief description of the population to be served by the proposed program.**

The populations to be served by our proposed project are our community of gardeners, volunteers, and students: Amicitia Community Gardens (ACG) Board of Directors, ACG staff, ACG sponsors, ACG funders, collaborative businesses and agencies, and the community-at-large that is made up of urban-dwelling families and individuals.

**Provide a complete description of your proposed project. Be sure to include how this project relates to fulfilling your organizational mission, the impact this project will have on your community, and your expected outcome at the completion of the grant.**

Amicitia Community Gardens (ACG) is, and has been, growing at an astounding rate over the past ten years. With the increased number of gardens we have begun in the city of Westview has come a great increase in the number of organizational stakeholders. These stakeholders include gardeners who tend our community gardens, backyard gardeners, volunteers, employees, and students, as well as community members who just want to see us flourish. While our numbers have grown, our ability to communicate with this ever-expanding stakeholder base has fallen behind.

*ACG is a community gardening cooperative whose mission is to assist families, neighborhoods, and organizations in growing food for themselves and the community. Amicitia Community Gardens is a friendly organization where all community members can come together to cultivate our connection to nature and each other by growing food locally. Amicitia Community Gardens envisions an environmentally educated community in which people of all ages and backgrounds are encouraged to learn how to garden, reconnect with the land, and connect with our community.*

*In a recent strategic plan, ACG has identified a number of objectives and activities aimed at bringing our communications network up to date. A specific organizational goal is to assist families in growing food for themselves. A specific measurable objective associated with this goal is the improvement of communications between families involved in ACG programs for a more open exchange of ideas and information. An activity that we are proposing is the expansion of the organizational Web site to include a family forum area for use by neighborhood family gardeners.*

*Another identified goal that we are working toward is to assist ACG member gardeners interested in the commercial options of gardening. Toward this goal, we have set as a specific measurable objective the organizing of an online seed sales initiative. To accomplish this objective and a part of this proposed project, we must engage in the activity of developing the ACG Web site to promote and facilitate seed sales.*

*To better communicate with all our members, it is our goal to expand the reach of our organizational newsletter. We realize that many members of our community, for a wide variety of reasons, do not use computers. To ensure that we are providing the best communication possible of ACG programs and services, we must expand our newsletter to communicate with our growing community of gardeners and friends.*

*Enhancing our communications tools relates to the fulfillment of our organizational mission as we enhance our ability to bring our community together through gardening. Enhancing our communications tools assists and encourages community members of all ages and backgrounds to reconnect with the land and to connect with our community.*

### Budget
*Amount requested: $15,000*
*Total project budget: $45,000*
*Total annual organization budget: $950,000*

*Is the implementation of this project dependent upon other pending requests?*
*Yes No*

*If yes, please indicate how the project would be affected if other pending requests are not funded. N/A*

Beyond this narrative section of the grant was a tool that Rose used to select her attachments to the proposal. A button that allowed Rose to submit her proposal appeared after she attached all the required documents. After she submitted the full proposal with documentation, Rose received a reference number that was followed by an e-mail notifying her that her proposal had been successfully submitted.

With this submittal, Rose had accomplished her task of submitting three grant proposals. The proposals had the possibility of bringing $120,000 to Amicitia Community Gardens over the following three fiscal years. All of the projects proposed were directly related to the mission of the organization and sprang from Amicitia Community Gardens' long-term strategic plan.

If you go back and carefully read Rose's proposals, you will see that most, if not all, of the information that she included in each aspect of her narratives came out of the early preparation she did. The preparation we examined in Section 1 of this book came in handy in preparing each of the individual proposals.

While some of the steps were not necessary to writing your grant proposal, you have just read how each of these steps was, ultimately, extremely useful.

Now that Rose has written three grant proposals, she is prepared to do many more as the occasions arise. She needs, though, to remember the fundamentals that she learned along the way:

- Have a constant eye on the mission and vision
- Keep the strategic plan up-to-date
- Ensure the objectives and activities in her plan are SMART
- Do research on prospective funders
- Utilize the organizations network

Though Rose felt the best about the Westview Community Foundation proposal, she felt good about each one she put together. She thought she did what was required and did so in a clear voice. She knows and believes in her organizational mission and vision. She eagerly looks forward to Amicitia Community Gardens' future.

## CASE STUDY: BRIAN WILLIAMS, VICE PRESIDENT OF DEVELOPMENT

The Children's Museum of Indianapolis
3000 North Meridian Street
Indianapolis, IN 46208
**www.childrensmuseum.org**

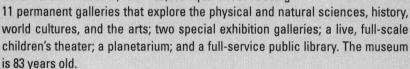

The Children's Museum of Indianapolis is the world's largest children's museum, with 433,000 square feet housing 11 permanent galleries that explore the physical and natural sciences, history, world cultures, and the arts; two special exhibition galleries; a live, full-scale children's theater; a planetarium; and a full-service public library. The museum is 83 years old.

I personally have been seeking/writing grants as the "lead" grant officer at the museum for less than one year. We seek funding from local, regional, and national funding organizations for a wide array of programs supported by our annual operating budget, as well as for exhibit construction and renovation, capital expansion projects, and planning grants to explore new ideas related to exhibits and/or programs. Our annual receipts from grant funding range from $500,000 to $5,000,000.

As a grant seeker, we look primarily to match the project proposed and the funding organization's interests. The Children's Museum also seeks to expand our reach nationally, and so targets nationally prominent organizations such as the Kresge Foundation, the MacArthur Foundation, NASA, NEA, NEH, etc.

The Children's Museum has a national and international reputation for being an industry leader in creating immersive exhibits and programs across the arts, sciences, and humanities that engage children and their families, as well as school group visitors. We have a proven record of success in providing an invaluable, informal learning environment that families and educators value as a quality experience for their children. The museum is at the cutting edge of immersive exhibit designs and construction that immerse the visitor in the experience and provide hands-on interaction throughout the galleries.

Words of wisdom to those who are new to seeking foundation funding: research, research, research. Make sure your proposals are strategic, targeted at the funding interests of the organizations that you are submitting to, compelling in their substantive content, and well-written. Be brief and to the point. Use short sentences and active verbs to ensure your proposal is among the most easy to read in the program officer's pile. Anticipate your reader's needs and provide answers in your presentation.

# Chapter 19

## Proposal Attachments

Before we continue in Rose's quest and find out what happened to her proposals, we should step back and look at the attachments that she submitted. Here is a list of all the attachments that were asked for in the proposals Rose submitted:

### *Financial Information*

- *Most recent audited financial statement. This information should include a balance sheet, statement of activities (or statement of income and expenses), and functional expenses.*
- *Organization budget for current year, including income and expenses*
- *Current (year-to-date) financial statements*
- *Project budget, including income and expenses (if request is for project support)*
- *Major contributors.*
- *In-kind contributions*
- *Your most recent IRS Form 990*
- *Explanation of items in financial attachments, if applicable*

### Other Attachments

- *Board of directors list*
- *A copy of your current IRS determination letter indicating tax-exempt 501(c) (3) status*
- *Key staff.*
- *Annual report, if available*
- *A letter from the executive officer of the financial agent on the financial agent's letterhead certifying their financial responsibility for the organization submitting the proposal. Include the following language:*

*"I certify that this organization, as fiscal agent, takes reasonable steps to ensure that grant funds are not ultimately distributed to terrorist organizations and that staff, board, and other volunteers have no dealings whatsoever with known terrorists or terrorist organizations."*

- *Statement of assurance signed by an officer of your organization (e.g., CEO, president, executive director, COO, CFO, comptroller, or treasurer) stating that all statements included herein are true*
- *Final report from most recent XYZ Foundation Grant (if applicable)*

At first glance, the list of financial information to be attached to a funding proposal can seem a bit overwhelming. However, you should be tracking much of this information regardless of whether you are preparing a grant proposal.

## Most Recent Audited Financial Statement

The top item on the list above is your most recent audited financial statement. This refers to that independently audited statement that was discussed in Chapter 5. You may be asked for your most recent statement, but you may also be asked for the past two or three independently audited statements.

Again, to have an independent auditor put the unbiased stamp of accountability, transparency, and compliance to accept accounting principals on your finances is to tell potential funders that you will also keep a close eye on the funds they grant you. If your organization has not had an independent audit done, it is worth your while to begin doing so. Any exploration of funding guidelines will show you that this is an item required in most proposals.

## Organization Budget for Current Year, Including Income and Expenses

This is another item that you should be able present without too much effort. Again, you may, on occasion, be asked for an expanded budget that might reflect a preliminary budget for the next fiscal year. When this is asked for, people understand that the budget is preliminary. This is often requested, as the project you propose may take place in the next fiscal year. It is important that you show how your project fits into your organizational budget.

Organizational budgets vary in format. Organizations often have budgets in a few different formats for use, depending on the situation. Organizational directors, such as executive directors and program directors, may deal with expansive budgets that lay the financial story out as completely as possible. Other budgets may be formatted for use at meetings of the board of directors that give clear thumbnail sketches of the budget. The budget you choose to submit with your funding proposal should be the one that gives the clearest picture in a most concise way.

## Current (year-to-date) Financial Statements

This document could be included as the same document noted above. Often, organizations will present a document that states the budget for the year alongside the current (year-to-date) financial statements. This gives them a good look at their projections and their current financial standing related to their forecasted finances. This document allows a foundation to see how well the organization is able to plan for the future.

## Project Budget, Including Income and Expenses (if request is for project support)

This is the first item that you will have to draw up as a direct result of your funding proposal. This is where you show the numbers proposed and reflect how the funding will fit into your overall budget.

This budget will be specific in a way that you may not have been in your overall organizational budget. Here, you will break down the specific income and expenses of the program you are proposing to the foundation.

The format of the project budget is optional if the foundation has not provided you with a budget form to fill out. Attach a budget narrative explaining your numbers if necessary.

Here is an example of a project budget for Amicitia Community Gardens' proposal to the XYZ Foundation. It is the proposed budget to hire and train part-time associate gardeners:

**INCOME**

| Source | Amount |
|---|---|
| *Support* | |
| Government grants | |
| Westview City Green Grant | $ 18,000 |
| Corporations | |
| HomeRite | $ 6,000 |

| Foundations | |
|---|---|
| The XYZ Foundation (this proposal) | $ 45,000 |
| Individual contributions | $ 9,000 |
| Fundraising events and products | $ 18,000 |
| Membership income | $ 25,920 |
| In-kind support | $ 4,500 |
| | |
| *Revenue* | $ |
| Earned income | $ |
| Other (specify) | $ |
| | |
| **Total Income** | **$ 126,420** |

## EXPENSES

| Item | Amount |
|---|---|
| Salaries and wages (break down by individual position and indicate full- or part-time) | |
| $6,000 x 3 | $ 18,000 |
| $6,000 x 6 | $ 36,000 |
| $6,000 x 9 | $ 54,000 |
| (see note associated w/this expense) | |
| SUBTOTAL | $108,000 |
| Travel | $ 1,800 |
| Equipment (shirts, hats, & gloves) | $ 270 |
| Laptop computers & associated software | $ 5,400 |
| In-kind expenses | $ 4,500 |
| Depreciation | $ 4,800 |
| Other (specify) | |
| | $ |
| Earned income | $ |
| Other (specify) | $ |
| | |

| Total Expense | $ 124,770 |
| Difference (Income less Expense) | $    1,650 |

**Notes Regarding Proposed Project Budget**

This budget spans the proposed three-year grant cycle.

**INCOME**

The grants indicated have been secured with the exception of this proposal. The Westview CityGreen Grant is the continuation and expansion of a grant that Amicitia Community Gardens has been receiving from the City of Westview for three years. The corporate grant from HomeRite is also the continuation and expansion of regular funding that Amicitia Community Gardens receives from the HomeRite Corporation. You will note on our Board of Directors list that our Board President is an officer of the HomeRite Corporation.

Individual contributions are anticipated from open garden celebrations that will be held as each of Amicitia Community Gardens' planned new gardens opens across the city over the next three years.

Amicitia Community Gardens holds two major fundraising events each year. Plans are for a percentage of funds generated through these events to be earmarked for this project.

Membership income reflects the growth in numbers of member gardeners that will come as a result of an increased number of community gardens and associate gardeners (AG).

In-kind support reflects gardening tools that are donated by the HomeRite Corporation.

## EXPENSES

Associate Gardeners are hired as independent contractors. A contract pays $6,000 annually. The expenses reflected in the proposed budget are for three new AGs the first year, with three more added the second year (for a total of six) and three added the third year (for a total of nine).

Each AG receives $100 annually for travel.

The budget example here is a budget for a specific program. Of course, the budget(s) you submit with your proposal will vary from this and be determined by the proposal itself. If you are seeking general operating support, the budget you submit may be exactly the same as your annual operating budget. If you are seeking support over several years, you may be required to submit budgets over the schedule of the grant period.

The individual that creates the budget determines the format of the budget example. Sometimes you will be provided with a budget template by the foundation you are applying to.

Rose set her budget up as a simple line item budget that indicates income, expenses, and a short narrative explaining a couple of items that she felt needed further definitions.

## Grant Seeking Tip

The things to consider as you put your budget together are to be clear, stick to the project, and be realistic. Every item in your budget should be directly associated with your project objectives and activities. If there is an item in your budget that is not associated with your project, your budget will be confusing and may even be seen as dishonest.

**INCOME**

Be prepared to spend as much time on your budget as you spend writing your narrative. Budget preparation can be a time-consuming task. After you get your budget together, be sure to have another pair of eyes proof it for clarity and precision.

| Source | Amount | Narrative |
|---|---|---|
| *Support* | | |
| Government grants | $ 18,000 | The Westview CityGreen Grant is the continuation and expansion of a grant that Amicitia Community Gardens has been receiving from the City of Westview for three years. |

## Major Contributors

Foundations want to know that they are not alone in their support of your organization. You may be wondering what you should do if you are new and have not gotten any major support to date. The answer? You must build relationships. You will read repeatedly in the case studies in this book that relationships are the most important part of this process. However, you still need to be prepared to voice your mission and vision, and you still are required to have a plan, a need, and a budget.

We will further explore this topic of building relationships later in the book, but for now, if you do not have any major contributors, do not panic — and do not make them up. Be truthful. While you may not have that individual or foundation that writes the check for $50,000, you might have 5,000 individuals that give you $10, which might be every bit as major and show just as much, if not more, support.

## In-kind Contributors

Expenses that are incurred on a no-payment basis are called in-kind expenses. For example, Amicitia Community Gardens needs specific tools to do the kind of gardening work they do. They could go to a store and purchase these tools, but instead, a local business donates them to the organization. That makes the expense of the tools — which Amicitia Community Gardens must show in their financial records — an in-kind expense. It is also shown on the income side of the budget as in-kind support. In-kind line items can include anything that can be identified as a legitimate cost to the project.

These contributions are crucial, as they can reflect the level of community and support for the organization, and can provide the leverage needed to access funding. As you consider the major contributors, do not forget that in-kind contributions can be major contributors as well.

Many organizations keep inadequate records of in-kind contributions. It is worth your while to talk to an accountant about establishing a system for the recording of such contributions. The important thing to take into account here is, once again, making your reporting of these contributions clear and realistic.

Here are a few more things to keep in mind about in-kind contributions:

- Identify and recognize contributors
- Record all in-kind contributions
- Do not forget that volunteer time and labor is a legitimate in-kind contribution
- Categorize all in-kind contributions

## IRS Form 990

We discussed Form 990 in Chapter 5. The IRS Form 990 is the return filed by organizations exempt from income tax, or not-for-profits. Some foundations may ask that you provide several years of IRS Form 990.

If you are a not-for-profit organization or have a pending application for not-for-profit status, you have a federal ID number that designates you as such. If you have this status, you should have a history of 990s. In some cases, if you are a new or young organization, you can get by without including audited financial statements by only adding your 990s to your grant proposal. If you have to go this route, talk to the foundation first. Remember, proposals may not be considered unless you have submitted all the required information.

## Explanation of Items in Financial Attachments, if applicable

You may need to provide an explanation of any of the financial items you have attached to your proposal. If you do so, keep your explanations clear and concise. If you have any questions about attachments, do not be afraid to ask the foundation. Take as much guess work out of your proposal as you can.

## *Other Attachments*

## Board of directors list

You should have in your files a list of your current board of directors. Some foundations will ask for a simple list of names; some foundations will ask for a list of names and contact information. Many foundations will ask for names, contact information, and board affiliation — that is, who they are and what they do. You should be prepared to submit any and all of this information.

## A copy of your current IRS determination letter indicating tax-exempt 501 (c) (3) status

This is an item that is almost non-negotiable as a must-have attachment. You may get by with a letter proving that you have a pending application to the IRS. You may, if you are seeking funding as an individual, not be required to file this item. However, most foundations will require that your organization be a tax-exempt entity.

As we discussed in Chapter 13, all 501(c) (3) organizations are further categorized as one of five types under IRC 509(a). Amicitia Community Gardens is recognized as 509(a) (1). This simply means that Amicitia Community Gardens is a publicly supported charity. Your organization may have a different sub-classification that will be found on your letter of determination from the IRS.

## Key staff

Like your board list, this list will indicate those on your staff who are instrumental in your organizational operations and will include names, positions, and contact information. You will also list staff members here who are instrumental in the proposed project.

## Annual report

If you compiled all the attachments that we have discussed thus far and packaged them as a single, easy-to-read package, you would have a complete annual report. Most small not-for-profit organizations do not compile annual reports, though most not-for-profit directors recognize the value annual reports can provide. A well-constructed annual report will help you display your accomplishments to current stakeholders, introduce your organization to prospective stakeholders, and recognize important people in your organizational circle.

Your annual report need not be a glossy, high-cost event. It is more important that it tells the story of your organization's work over the past year; whether you do that in a four-page ring binder or a glossy, bound, and five-color extravaganza is your choice.

The most essential part of a not-for-profit annual report is the description of your achievements. You want to be sure to tell potential funders what you did, but more importantly, you want to explain why you did it. Explore your strategic plan and let the reader of your annual report see that you achieved some of your objectives. Tell the reader what the outcomes were. An annual report explains how your activities affected your organization and your community. Your annual report should tell the story of how your activities helped you achieve your mission.

Your annual report should contain:

- The financial information that you have been asked to include in your proposal
- Audited financial statement
- A list of contributors, board of directors, and staff members
- Anything that tells the story of how your organization fared over the year
- A letter from the executive officer of the fiscal agent on the fiscal agent's letterhead certifying their fiscal responsibility for the organization submitting the proposal (And/or) A statement of assurance signed by an officer of your organization (e.g., CEO, president, executive director, COO, CFO, comptroller, or treasurer) stating that all statements included herein are true

Often, the individual writing the grant proposal is not the chief executive of the organization, or the organization is a partner or umbrella organization seeking funding for a member organization. What a foundation needs to see with these statements is assurance that the chief executive is aware of the proposed request, signs off on all statements and attachments, and is taking responsibility for the administration of any funding that may be provided.

## Final report from most recent grant (if applicable)

This is an attachment that Rose and Amicitia Community Gardens do not have to worry about at this point, but it will become an issue as grants start being made. Most foundations want to see an assessment of the program they fund. They want to see, precisely, how their funds were used. Most foundations ask to see this assessment before they give more financial support to an organization.

Final reports will vary from foundation to foundation — like the grant applications — but most, if not all, final reports demand an assessment of the program, project, or general operation funds that were granted.

## Executive Summary

An executive summary is a short explanation of a proposal. It is a document that, if required, is placed at the beginning of the grant proposal. The format of the executive summary is quite similar to a letter of intent in that it will contain much of the same information. In your executive summary, you will want to briefly touch on these points:

- Project/Program definition
- Proposed project link to foundation's priorities
- Project need
- Project outcomes
- Project budget
- Type of grant you request and amount requested
- Organizational qualifications

It is important to remember that this is a summary and that you need to keep it brief. You should attempt to clearly define all of the above points in a page or less.

## Articles of incorporation

If you are seeking foundation funding as a not-for-profit corporation, you have gone though the process of incorporating and applying to the IRS for your status. Even if you have a pending case before the IRS, you have become incorporated. As such, you should have articles of incorporation.

Articles of incorporation is the legal paperwork that you file with your state — probably with the office of the secretary of state — in which you state that you were forming a business within the state, and that you filed with the intent of being a tax-exempt corporation. This is a necessary step to take before you apply with the IRS for federal tax-exempt status.

## Organizational by-laws

If you are a recognized, registered not-for-profit corporation, you have by-laws. By-laws are the legal documents that tell your organization or, more precisely, your board of directors, how to conduct its affairs.

By-laws are documents that you probably had to file with your state when you formed your organization. Because laws vary from state to state, you probably consulted with an attorney as you started your organization and constructed your by-laws.

## Letters of support

You will be asked to supply foundations with letters from stakeholders expressing their support of you organization. If the foundation asks for these, try to supply them with letters that express a wide array of your stakeholder constituency. Amicitia Community Gardens might supply letters from board members, gardeners, students, and the community-at-large.

## Articles, brochures, pictures

These are documents of your work. Some of this documentation may be from your organization's public relations mechanisms, and some may be from local newspapers and/or community organizations' newsletters.

## Additional attachments

Whatever it is that you are asked to include, if you do not or cannot provide the foundation with a specific item, contact the foundation and explain your situation — do not just omit it. Doing so will likely be a waste of your time and grant writing efforts, as grant applications that are incomplete will not be considered. Make sure you read the foundation guidelines thoroughly to be sure you are attaching everything required. There may be some additional documents requested specifically from a particular foundation.

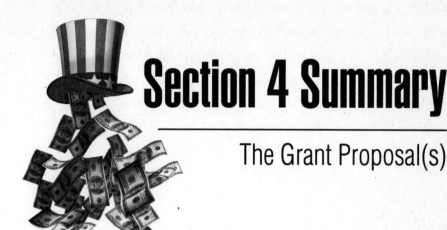

# Section 4 Summary

## The Grant Proposal(s)

You will notice that whether you are asked to fill in a grant form on paper, write a grant narrative, or fill in an online application, you have to be prepared with many of the same materials from grant to grant. What changes is your needs statement.

You have been reading case studies as you have gone through this book. Many of the individuals that have stated their thoughts and experiences with grant seeking have stressed the importance of building relationships. You saw in the example of Rose's grant proposal to the Westview Community Foundation that her relationship with the foundation came about out of an established relationship through her board of directors. The point is that even though she submitted her proposal to a foundation that knew of her organization, she still had to make a case for funding. She would have had to make a case for funding even if the foundation had told her there was no paperwork involved and she made her proposal over lunch with a foundation director.

The most important thing you can take away from this section of the book is the need to be prepared to tell your story. Be prepared to state your need and show how you fit into your community; understand the vision of your organization as well as the vision of the foundation you are seeking funding from. If this is done, the act of writing — or speaking about — your proposal should be a relatively easy task.

# Section 5

## Post Proposal

N ow that the proposals are written and compiled, you may want to sit back and relax, but wait. Did you do everything properly? Did you get all the attachments? How are you going to submit your proposal? We covered this all in passing earlier as we followed Rose in preparing Amicitia Community Gardens' proposals, but let us further explore some of these post-writing/compilation tasks. In this section, we will explore the in-house editing process and various ways to package and submit your proposals.

# Chapter 20

## The In-House Editing Process

We have seen, as we followed Amicitia Community Gardens' proposal process, that as Rose wrote and compiled her proposals, she would turn them over to several individuals to be looked at. This is a crucial step, as this editing process is vital to putting together a proposal that is clear and complete.

Rose designated two people who represent her organization to look at her proposals. She chose a staff member who is involved with the organization on a day-to-day basis to look at the proposal from one point of view, and she selected a board member to examine the proposal from another point of view. While this level of editing is not required of foundations, it is a level of security that you are advised to employ if you are new to grant seeking.

If you are a young organization that is new to this process, a board member's knowledge, experience, and opinions in these matters are vital. But it is also essential that board members understand the process of grant seeking. You are helping each other to help your organization.

The truth of the matter is that your board of directors is the legal bottom line of your organization; they are the responsible body. In looking at attachments in the last chapter, we touched on articles of incorporation and bylaws. In most cases, what these documents say is that the board of directors is responsible for the activities; for fulfilling the mission of the organization; and for seeing to it that it is done in a legal, responsible manner. As such, it is vital that the board understand this aspect of the organizational business. To understand what the organization is involved in as it seeks potentially thousands of dollars in funding, members of the board should read and understand the requests. If there is anything about the proposal that the board member does not understand or agree with, it is vital that the individual preparing the proposal rethink how the request is being made and what is being asked.

Here is a checklist of things that your in-house editing staff should take into account. That is, as Rose's co-worker read her proposals, these are the items that were given close attention:

- Spelling
- Grammar
- Math
- Proper formatting
- Clarity of request
- Persuasiveness
- Conciseness of narrative
- Whether the proposal matched the guidelines
- That all attachments accounted for
- Complete final reports (if so, run the checklist of them)
- Correct contact information
- Properly addressed proposal

You might even offer a more precise, measurable review sheet that your co-worker can score your work with. You can offer this review sheet to several individuals to gain an idea of how your proposals come across. Note that the first items scored measure the SMART points of the proposal:

# Example Proposal Review Sheet

Please review the grant proposal using the following scale for each standard specified below:

4 = Excellent      2 = Average

3 = Good      1 = Poor

_____ **Specificity**

Grant proposal shows a real need and uses relevant support data

_____ **Measurability**

Actionable objectives for the proposed program are clear, concise, and measurable.

_____ **Achievability**

The proposal is written in such as way as to show that the project/program can be done by the organization as it is outlined and stated.

_____ **Realism**

The proposal and the attached documentation propose a project/program that the organization can realistically achieve with its existing resources or with the assistance of the identified foundation.

_____ **Timeliness**

The proposal shows that the investment in this work is urgent and the organizational history and strategic plan reinforce the timeliness of the request.

_____ **Organizational credibility**

The organization has clearly shown that it has experience in and credibility for the kind of work detailed in the grant proposal.

**Staffing**

The organization has clearly shown it has human resources necessary to carry out the proposed program

**Participation**

The grant proposal clearly defines how stakeholders will participate in the overall implementation of the program.

**Collaboration**

The grant proposal clearly documents and defines the roles of collaborative partners that will be a part of the program.

**Assessment plan**

There is a clear assessment plan.

**Sustainability**

The project is sustainable, and the sustainability is clearly defined and documented.

**Funder fit**

The program/project is clearly linked to the funder's priorities.

**Proposal clarity, organization, and completeness**

The grant proposal is organized in the manner stated in the grant guidelines. The writing is clear and concise; ideas are stated in a logical progression. The funder guidelines for contents of the proposal, and attachments are followed.

**Visual Presentation**

The grant proposal is neat and easy to follow and read.

TOTAL SCORE: _____ /56

**COMMENTS:**

You can perform an exercise by going back to Rose's proposals and scoring them based on the above criteria. Doing exercises such as this can help you understand what works and what does not work in putting grant proposals together. If you have been working along with Rose and writing a proposal or exercise proposal, try reviewing your own work with this checklist. Better yet, give your proposal and this checklist to someone with a fresh set of eyes and have them look it over. Even with this checklist in hand, it is often difficult to score your own work, as you have been staring at it for some time and are used to seeing and reading things in a set way.

After the work has been read and scored, re-examine the items that scored low and do what you can to clarify them. Have the individual that scored the proposal offer suggestions as to what you might do to clarify. Often, the act of asking the right question will help you start thinking in the right direction.

After the items that score low are restated, ask the person who originally scored it to look it over again and check that you solved your problem. Perhaps you can have another individual read the proposal to see how you fare with a new perspective. Having more than one person check and even double-check your proposal will ensure that it is written coherently and includes the proper content.

# Chapter 21

## Submission and Beyond

N ow you have everything written, checked, and compiled. The final question that should be answered before you submit your proposal is: How will you package your proposal?

Rose's proposal to the Herald Charitable Foundation was simple in that all she needed do was click a "submit" button. Beyond that, your options are seemingly limited. Think about that question from the funder's perspective. Make it easy for those who read your proposal to do so.

A well-formatted proposal will:

- Be printed on white paper in a font and point size that is easy to read
- Have the correct line spacing and page borders, as per the funder's guidelines
- Include page numbers on every page
- Have the name on the organization and program/project in the header or footer of each page
- Be organized according to the listed in the guidelines.
- Have the requested copies of all documents

After your proposal is organized, decide how you will keep it all together. Do not staple your proposal. If a funder asks that the proposal be bound in a specific way, follow those directions. If there is not a specified manner of binding, you can bind it with a binder clip, put it in a folder, or have it bound at an office store — whatever you feel will give your proposal the best look.

The last thing you should do prior to delivery is ensure you have a copy for your records. You might even want to retain multiple copies for your records. Keep the copies in the same format and order that you deliver them in.

Your delivery options are not as varied as your packaging options, but you do have choices if you have not submitted electronically. If you are submitting a proposal to a local foundation, you might consider hand-delivering your proposal. Hand delivery gives you the assurance of knowing that your proposal has not gotten lost in the mail and that it arrived on time. If you choose to hand-deliver your proposal, be sure that you obtain a receipt from the person you hand it to.

If you choose to have your proposal delivered another way, such as the U.S. Postal Service, FedEx, UPS, or another service, be sure that you:

- Can track your package
- Ask for guaranteed delivery
- Ask for a confirmation of receipt
- Make sure that a street address and phone number of the recipient is included
- Avoid delivering the proposal to a post office (PO) box

Finally, keep track of all your proposals. Keep a file for each foundation you apply to, and keep a record of when you submitted your proposal.

You have done quite a bit of work to get to this point of submitting this funding proposal, and as you hand your proposal off to a foundation, it is natural to wonder if you will be awarded the grant. At this point, there is not much you can do but wait. Do not call the foundation on a weekly basis to find out whether you were approved; let them call you.

The foundation may call you before the decision is made with questions about your proposal, or they may call to request a site visit to your organization. Be prepared for these situations, and inform your staff that this is a possibility.

It is good to know that if you are not approved for funding, you are ready to knock on more doors and that, eventually, if you are persistent, you will be successful. If you have a good product and you knock on enough doors, perseverance can prove effective.

## CASE STUDY: MARY LAURA JONES, FOUNDING BOARD MEMBER

International Consultants & Associates (IC&A)

1454 W. Fargo Avenue

Chicago, IL 60626

**www.icanda.org**

IC&A has been around since 2006 and funds support and training for African-based organizations in 11 countries that work on preventative HIV/AIDS programs. I am an IC&A Board member and have been writing grants for 25 years.

I search primarily for grants from government and family foundations. I am involved in researching and securing special program funding. As a result of our foundation relationships, we receive $30,000 - $60,000 annually. The funds we receive are typically for unique, timely projects and programs.

I think that a grant proposal is made compelling through personal contact ahead of writing the proposal. Sit down with a foundation representative who advises what they are looking for in a proposal and what areas they wish to fund. As a grant seeker, I look for foundations that display compassion and interest in international HIV/AIDS prevention. What funders find attractive about IC&A is that we support indigenous staffs to do important innovative programs around a life-and-death issue in Africa.

For those who are new to seeking foundation funding, my words of wisdom are: relationships, relationships, relationships; visits, visits, visits. Personal contact is the key to any foundation funding.

# Part 2 Summary

In Part Two, you took all of the research and organization you did in Part One and put it on paper. We explored a variety of proposal application forms and formats, as well as many of the attachments you might be asked for as part of your funding proposal.

After you have written and compiled a handful of grant proposals, you will become accustomed to the process and will more easily know what to expect from foundation to foundation. You will gain more assurance and understanding of what is expected from you — and what you might expect from foundations.

However, do not become complacent. Keep doing your research. Hold to the fundamentals of your organizational mission and vision.

Keep track of your calendar, and do not try to rush your grant writing. Always give yourself plenty of time to compose and compile your materials. Always try to give your organization time to properly check and re-check your proposals.

Keep track of your calendar, and be sure that you are not attempting to package and submit your proposal on the last day at the last minute. Mistakes can easily happen this way.

Remember, the proposal goes beyond what you put on paper. Every chance you get to build a relationship with a prospective funder, do it. Often, the proposal you submit to a foundation is a way to introduce your organization. You may not get the grant, but you have introduced yourself. This is important. It may take numerous proposals to a foundation before they approve one, but, all the while, they are learning about your organization. Do not get discouraged. If you have done your research and the foundation you are approaching with a funding proposal is a good match, they will eventually take notice of you. In the next section, you will see what an organization should do if awarded, denied, or only partially awarded a grant.

# PART THREE

## Now What?

You have researched your organization; you have researched the foundations and identified those that might become partners in your mission. You have written, budgeted, received, and packaged your proposals. Now we arrive at Part 3 of the book, which reviews various scenarios that may occur after your proposal has been submitted. The chapters in *Now What?* examine stewardship of foundation funding. They will also cover what happens if you are awarded funding, denied funding, or awarded partial funding. Take a close look at how Rose handles herself in each situation. No matter what happens with your proposal, it is important to handle yourself with diplomacy.

# Section 6

## Stewardship

Stewardship refers to the way you manage your relationship with a foundation. This is important, regardless of whether your proposal is approved. It may take several proposals submitted over the course of two or three years before you are funded by a particular foundation. Consequently, how you manage your relationship with each foundation you submit proposals to is important. It is a mistake to think that stewardship is important only if you receive the grant; it is equally as important if you have been denied funding or if only partial funding has been awarded. As you read through Rose's actions in each situation, pay close attention to how she treats each of the foundations.

# Chapter 22

## Funding Awarded or Denied

It was not too long after Rose sent her funding proposal to the Westview Community Foundation that she received a call from Robert Town, the executive director of the foundation. Mr. Town expressed his thanks for the proposal and informed Rose that Amicitia Community Gardens' proposal had been approved for funding. He informed her that she would soon be receiving a letter informing her of the award, along with a funding agreement (contract) that will spell out the specifics of how the funding can be used. Mr. Town also invited Rose and her staff to attend an awards luncheon to officially announce the new partnership to the community of Westview.

After this phone call, Rose felt energized. She now felt certain that all of her funding proposals would be accepted, though she was surprised at how quickly the Westview Community Foundation had made their decision to fund Amicitia Community Gardens' project.

Now Rose needed to re-open her file on the Westview Community Foundation. The first addition to her file was a thank-you letter to the Westview Community Foundation for the grant award. It read:

# Sample Thank-you Letter

Amicitia Community Gardens
Rose Flowers, Executive Director

Robert Town
Executive Director
Westview Community Foundation
P.O. Box 789
Westview, IN 46322

Dear Mr. Town:

Amicitia Community Gardens would like to thank the Westview Community Foundation for the generous capacity-building grant awarded. We are excited that you believe in and share the mission and vision of our organization, and we look forward to working as partners with you to make Westview a green and healthy community.

We gratefully acknowledge and accept the grant awarded, and we plan on attending the award announcement and celebration that you have planned. We are eager to get to know you and the other grant award recipients of our community.

Again, we thank you for your consideration, and we look forward to working with you.

Sincerely,
Rose Flowers
Executive Director
Amicitia Community Gardens

## Grant Seeking Tip

The thank-you letter accomplishes two tasks. It is a simple thank-you for the award, and it acts as an informal acceptance of the grant. The more formal acceptance is in the form of the ceremonial acceptance that will occur at the celebration and the signing of the contract.

Rose dropped the thank-you letter in the mail and waited to get the award letter that Mr. Town spoke of, along with the contract. The contract was not long in coming. The award contract was a simple, fairly common document outlining the agreement Amicitia Community Gardens was to make with the Westview Community Foundation. Attached to the contract was a copy of the proposed capacity-building grant that Rose had written. What follows is a standard, simple legal contract that you may see as you begin to receive positive responses from your grant proposals.

# Sample Grant Award Contract

*The undersigned "Grantee" (organization) accepts the grant made by the Westview Community Foundation (the "Foundation") by grant award notification dated _____. The Grantee agrees as follows:*

*1. No part of this grant, or any income received with respect thereto, shall be used for any purpose other than the purposes specified in the Foundation's Grant Proposal (included as an attachment to this contract).*

*2. No part of this grant shall be expended (a) to carry on propaganda or otherwise attempt to influence legislation within the meaning of Section 4945(d) (1) of the Internal Revenue Code, or (b) to influence the outcome of any specific public election or carry on, directly or indirectly, any voter registration drive except as permitted by section 4945(f).*

3. *No part of this grant shall be used for any purpose other than one specified in section 170(c) (2) (B) of the Internal Revenue Code.*

4. *The Grantee shall furnish to the Foundation a full and complete annual report describing the manner in which the grant funds were spent and the progress that was made in accomplishing the purposes of the grant.*

5. *The Grantee shall furnish to the Foundation a full and complete final report describing the manner in which grant funds were spent and the outcomes of the designated award at the end of the grant cycle, as defined in the attached proposal.*

6. *The Foundation may, at its expense, monitor and conduct an evaluation of operations funded by this grant, which may include visits by Foundation representatives to observe the Grantee's program procedures and operations, as well as discussions concerning the program with Grantee's personnel.*

7. *There must be an accurate and complete financial record, kept by the grantee, of expenses and funds received during the terms of the grant for at least three years after all grant funds are fully expended. The Foundation may, at its expense and on reasonable notice to the Grantee, audit or have audited the Grantee's records as they relate to the activities funded by this grant.*

8. *Any unexpended award monies, at the completion of the proposed project, are to be returned to the foundation.*

9. The Grantee will provide appropriate publicity concerning this grant and will allow the Foundation to review and approve the text of any publicity concerning this grant prior to the release of such publicity.

10. Grantee hereby acknowledges that it did not provide any goods or services to the Foundation, its officers, directors, or agents in consideration of this grant.

11. The total amount of this grant, or any portion thereof, may be discontinued, modified, or withheld at any time when, in the judgment of the Foundation, such action is necessary to comply with the requirements of any law or regulation affecting the Foundation's responsibilities with respect to this grant, or if the grantee fails in the opinion of the foundation to make progress toward the intended goals as outlined in the grant letter.

12. The Grantee shall immediately notify the Foundation in writing if: (a) its exemption is revoked, (b) it has any reasonable grounds to believe its exemption may be revoked, (c) any change is made or proposed to the Grantee's classification as an organization described in section 509(a) (1), (2), or (3) of the Internal Revenue Code or as a private operating Foundation, or it has any reasonable grounds to believe any such change may be made, or (d) the Grantee believes that it cannot continue to expend the grant in the manner designated in the Foundation's grant award letter.

If the Foundation does not receive the countersigned copy of this agreement within fourteen (14) days of mailing, the approved grant can be revoked. The grant payment will be mailed once the contract agreement is received.

The Grantee acknowledges that it has received and retained a copy of this Agreement. The undersigned hereby certifies that he or she is duly authorized to *accept this grant on behalf of the Grantee and to commit the Grantee to all of its terms and conditions.*

Rose read and understood most of the contract sent to her by the Westview Community Foundation, but there were a few things that she needed to clarify before she signed off on the document.

You may remember the research that Rose had to do regarding IRS codes when she was reading funding guidelines. Rose's research focused on the definition of charitable organizations, and it was determined by the IRS code 501(c) (3) and 509(a) (1, 2, or 3). This contract threw a few more IRS codes her way that she needed clarification on.

Paragraph 2 reads, "No part of this grant shall be expended (a) to carry on propaganda or otherwise attempt to influence legislation within the meaning of Section 4945(d) (1) of the Internal Revenue Code, or (b) to influence the outcome of any specific public election or carry on, directly or indirectly, any voter registration drive except as permitted by section 4945(f)."

Section 4945 of the tax code refers to monies spent by not-for-profits to carry on propaganda, or otherwise attempt to influence legislation, including grass-roots lobbying and direct lobbying by communicating to the general public.

Private foundations must also ensure that a grant earmarked for a voter registration project meets several additional requirements to avoid having the grant or activity classified as a taxable expenditure. In part, these requirements — found in Section 4945(f) — require voter registration activities to be carried out by a Section 501(c)(3) organization over more than one election cycle and in at least five states.

Paragraph 3 of the contract reads: No part of this grant shall be used for any purpose other than one specified in section 170(c) (2) (B) of the Internal Revenue Code. Rose discovered that this part of the IRS code deals with charitable contributions. Specifically, the code reads:

"(c) Charitable contribution defined for purposes of this section, the term "charitable contribution" means a contribution or gift to or for the use of — (2) A corporation, trust, or community chest, fund, or foundation —(B) organized and operated exclusively for religious, charitable, scientific, literary, or educational purposes, or to foster national or international amateur sports competition (but only if no part of its activities involve the provision of athletic facilities or equipment), or for the prevention of cruelty to children or animals."

Rose, after clarifying the points of the contract she was uncertain about, shared the contract with her board of directors and signed it. The grant was awarded, the contract signed, and Amicitia Community Gardens planned to move forward with the project. They also planned to move forward with their new relationship with the Westview Community Foundation.

Rose was determined to move forward in the proposed project and in this new relationship in a most responsible manner. She was quite certain that the relationship with the foundation would suffer if the project failed because of lack of follow-through or mismanagement of any kind. She knew as she signed the contract that she, her staff, and the board of directors had to work hard to be successful with every aspect of the proposal and contract. She also understood the importance of communication with the Westview Community Foundation.

Rose began a checklist of things she felt she needed to do to keep the foundation in the loop regarding the capacity-building project they were involved in.

- Do more than just put the foundation on the mailing list. Make a special effort to provide the foundation with regular updates on Amicitia Community Gardens' activities.

- Invite foundation directors to visit Amicitia Community Gardens. Invite foundation directors and staff to start a garden plot. It is important that the foundation see its money at work.

- Invite foundation directors to communicate with the community gardeners that are directly impacted by Amicitia Community Gardens and foundation actions.

## Grant Seeking Tip

There are many ways you can creatively involve a foundation in your activities. The important thing is to recognize the importance of their contribution.

## Making a Public Announcement about the Grant Award

Sometimes, it is important to make a public announcement of a foundation grant. If there is no mention of an announcement in your contract, the announcement may be made by the foundation itself. You may also consider printing a press release regarding the grant award. If you plan on putting together a press release related to a funding announcement, you should clear it with the awarding foundation prior to releasing it.

## *Sample Grant Award Announcement Press Release*

*Amicitia Community Gardens is proud to announce the receipt of a multi-year capacity-building grant for $60,000 from the Westview Community Foundation. The capacity-building initiative that Amicitia Community Gardens and the Westview Community Foundation will partner in will establish at least one community garden in each precinct of the city within the next three years. The fulfillment of this capacity-building initiative will call on Amicitia Community Gardens to establish nine community gardens in nine precincts of the city over the next three years.*

*Amicitia Community Gardens is a community gardening cooperative whose mission is to assist families, neighborhoods, and organizations in growing food for themselves and the community. Amicitia Community Gardens is a friendly organization where all community members can come together to cultivate our connection to nature and each other by growing food locally. Amicitia Community Gardens envisions an environmentally educated community in which people of all ages and backgrounds are encouraged to learn how to garden, reconnect with the land, and connect with our community.*

*The Westview Community Foundation believes that communities that work together create the kinds of communities that are worth living and raising children in. Through their grant-making programs, they support nonprofit organizations and community institutions that are improving our community in many different ways.*

*Amicitia Community Gardens is excited to move into the future with the Westview Community Foundation as a valued partner. If you have any questions about Amicitia Community Gardens or its programs, you can contact Rose Flowers, Amicitia Community Gardens' Executive Director. This press release is simple and to-the-point. It announces the award, recognizes the newly established community partnership, and defines both Amicitia Community Gardens and the Westview Community Foundation. It invites public questions, comment, and participation. With a press release such as this, Rose hopes not only to announce the grant award, but also to garner more interest in Amicitia Community Gardens and its programs.*

*Because our focus here is not on the program or project that Amicitia Community Gardens is involved in, but on the grant cycle and relationship they have begun with various foundations, we will look ahead to the future to see the continued relationship with the Westview Community Foundation. We will monitor what becomes of their other proposals — to the XYZ Foundation and the Herald Charitable Foundation — as well. But for now, we will look three years into the future to the time when the grant cycle with the Westview Community Foundation draws to a close.*

## Submitting a Final Report

Rose considered Amicitia Community Gardens' relationship with the Westview Community Foundation to be a solid one. Foundation board members had been to many Amicitia Community Gardens events. Some foundation staff members had volunteered to work in some of the gardens. Amicitia Community Gardens had accomplished the goals set forth in the capacity-building proposal. The gardens were established in each of the city precincts.

The time had come for Rose and Amicitia Community Gardens to step back and look at the three-year period and the capacity that had been built in the course of this grant cycle. Stepping back and looking at what had happened was a part of the organization's assessment mechanism, as well as the final task as outlined in the contract Amicitia Community Gardens had made with the Westview Community Foundation:

*The Grantee shall furnish to the Foundation a full and complete final report describing the manner in which grant funds were spent and the outcomes of the designated award at the end of the grant cycle as defined in the attached proposal.*

## Sample Final Report

### The Westview Community Foundation – Grantee Final Report

*This Grantee final report is designed to assist the Westview Community Foundation in better understanding the organizations we fund and to give those organizations an opportunity to assess their performance, share information about the programs they are involved in, and reflect upon their growth.*

The Westview Community Foundation also requests this final report comply with IRS regulations for grant-making foundations.

## Report Process for Grantee

*Any not-for-profit organizations receiving grants must provide annual reports and a final report at the end of a grant cycle.*

*If foundation funding is for one year, only one report is necessary.*

*Please keep your written summary to no more than three pages.*

## Guidelines for Reporting

*Grantee Report Form*

*Please e-mail your report to WCFoundation@WCFoundation.org or mail it to:*

*Westview Community Foundation*
*P.O. Box 789*
*Westview, IN 46322*


*Organization: <u>Amicitia Community Gardens</u>*
*Executive Director: <u>Rose Flowers</u>*
*Person reporting: <u>Rose Flowers</u>*
*Title: Executive: <u>Director</u>*
*e-mail: <u>rosie@organization.org</u>*


*Date of grant: <u>April 22, 2009</u>*
*Amount of grant: <u>$60,000</u>*
*Have all the grant funds been spent?*
*___ No, this is an interim report*
*<u>X</u> Yes, this is a final report*

## Grantee Report Narrative

*Please review and include your original grant proposal and grant agreement.*

*State the purpose of the grant. Please include a statement about the population served during the grant period.*

The grant awarded to Amicitia Community Gardens by the Westview Community Foundation was a capacity-building project that had been outlined in and a primary objective of Amicitia Community Gardens' long-term strategic plan. The primary organizational goal was to further develop the Community Garden Initiative. Toward that goal, and the project we engaged in, was to establish at least one community garden in each precinct of the city over three years.

The population that was most directly served was the community of gardeners that live in the city precincts where the new gardens were established. The students who attend Westview Public Schools in the neighborhoods where these new gardens were planted were also served. Indirectly served was the community-at-large, as these gardens were located in neighborhood lots that were designated as blighted.

*Describe the activities the organization engaged in to accomplish the objectives identified in the grant proposal.*
The fulfillment of this capacity-building initiative called upon Amicitia Community Gardens to establish nine community gardens in nine precincts of the city over the three-year period.

To accomplish our objective, Amicitia Community Gardens secured land on which to establish the gardens, made tools and sundry gardening necessities (such as seed, soil, and fertilizer) available for gardeners, recruited and trained volunteer gardeners, and hired and trained gardening associates.

Amicitia Community Gardens established two new gardens in the third and fifth precincts in the first year of the initiative. Gardens were planted in the seventh, eighth, and ninth precincts in the following spring. Planting the final four precincts, the 13th, 17th, 18th, and 20th, took place this past spring.

*To what extent were the intended activities accomplished?*
We had intended to establish nine community gardens over a three-year period in city precincts where there were no community gardens. At the end of the three-year period, there would be a community garden in every precinct of Westview. Amicitia Community Gardens accomplished the intended activates.

*Briefly describe any collaborative efforts or partnerships involved in planning or implementing this project.*

Amicitia Community Gardens has an excellent working relationship with the City of Westview and has been fortunate that the city places a high value on the work that Amicitia Community Gardens is doing. The city has been and continues to be a valuable partner, as they worked with us to identify locations in city neighborhoods that would be compatible with our activities. These locations not only include garden spots, but locations for potential farmers' markets, as well.

Amicitia Community Gardens also considers all of the neighborhood gardeners who have worked so hard with us to establish all of our gardens as valuable partners. Without the collaboration of the people in each precinct of Westview, our work would have proved untenable.

*Briefly describe the expected outcomes of the project.*

As Amicitia Community Gardens had proposed a capacity-building initiative that called upon the organization to establish community gardens, we have had to assess the project on two different levels. To achieve our objectives and build capacity, we expected to establish a community garden in each precinct of the city. This objective was met.

Primarily, we have had to assess the capacity building focus of our project. As we had expected, the establishment of the nine gardens has had a positive impact of the growth and long-term goals of our organization.

*Briefly describe the extent to which these expected outcomes have been realized.*

Growth has come as we have increased the number of gardens and stakeholders involved in our organization. We have seen growth in funding from earned and unearned revenue sources.

*Briefly describe the unexpected outcomes (positive or negative) that resulted from the project.*

Amicitia Community Gardens has had an unexpected growth in interest from "backyard" gardeners from all over the city as a result of our increase in visibility. We are in the process of enhancing our ability to assist these gardeners, as they have always been a part of our vision, but we were not prepared for the number of these gardeners who have approached us for assistance in a variety of different ways. Thus, this unexpected growth has been both a positive outcome and a negative one.

*Briefly describe the strengths and weaknesses of the project. Please detail how your organization addressed project weaknesses.*

The primary weakness of the project was that, from the beginning, it was tied closely to another grant-funded initiative. This, though it could have been a strength, proved to be a weakness because the project was only partially funded. The funding was to be for associate gardeners who were to work part-time in the new community gardens.

The organization's staff turned to our vast volunteer base for support, which was one of our strengths. A volunteer call was put out to enlist a group of specialized volunteer gardeners that have the knowledge and experience necessary to serve temporary posts as volunteer associate gardeners.

*Please identify changes that were made in the project plan.*

Other than the personnel matter listed above, no changes were made to our proposed plan.

*Briefly describe your plan for project sustainability.*

Amicitia Community Gardens has been working diligently to construct a many-tiered, dynamic development mechanism. We continuously work to expand our circle of stakeholders who work and act as volunteers, contributors, and supporters of our mission. We, our organization and community gardeners, have begun several commercial ventures that will assist in supporting not only our gardeners, but our organization as well. Through our growing farmers' markets and our increasing relationships with restaurants in the city, we are seeing an increase in our earned income. Our growing reputation as a well-grounded community organization is generating a great deal of interest from the funding community. This interest is helping us to see growth in our unearned income.

Besides the financial support we have seen from individual donors and from charitable foundations such as the Westview Community Foundation, we have noted a large increase in in-kind support over the past three years. Home Supply stores, Vantage Superstores, and Westview Home Improvement have all been valuable in-kind contributors to our community gardens.

Our continued growth and efforts to build a support network have been extremely fruitful, and we expect our gardens to continue to flourish well into the future.

## ATTACHMENTS
### *Please attach the following materials to this final report:*

1. Original grant proposal that includes original budget (it is not necessary to include all attachments requested in original grant)
2. Copy of signed grant agreement
3. Final project budget
4. Most recent audited financial statement
5. Brochures, pictures, and/or news articles related to project

The sample final report, as shown above, is just one of a multitude of formats you may come across. However, most will require much of the same information. The foundations want to know how their money was spent and what impact the grant made on the organization and the community it serves.

If your project was successful and did not deviate too much from the initial proposal, a final report is relatively easy to put together. Note that Rose, in writing her final report to the Westview Community Foundation, used much of the same language that she used in her proposal.

Things can be quite different, however, if your project runs into difficulties. If that happens, and things do not turn out exactly as planned, you should have defined the causes of the changes in any assessment process that you went through. Whatever you do, be truthful with the foundation. Understanding the mishaps is as important to them as it is to you.

You may have discovered a problem halfway into the project and had to alter your plans. If so, be as detailed about your changes as you can. As you develop a new strategy, do not be afraid to contact the funder to discuss your thoughts for change.

It is a mistake to think that if you turn in a final report that does not mirror your initial proposal, you will never get funding from this foundation again. With the final report, the foundations are interested in seeing an honest appraisal of your project. They are well-aware that things do not always go according to plan. The most important thing to remember as you enter a partnership like this is that you administer the project to the best of your abilities and keep the lines of communication open with your foundation partner. The final report is a way to put a cap on this administration and, ideally, is just a signpost along the road to a growing partnership.

# Funding is Denied

Sometimes it happens. Sometimes the proposal is denied and the organization does not receive funding from a foundation it has submitted a proposal to. If this happens to you, do not give up your search for funding. Continue looking; there is funding available for you somewhere.

Now let us take a look at what Rose does when her proposal is denied. We will start this scenario with an e-mail that Rose received from the Herald Charitable Foundation.

*Dear Ms. Flowers:*

*We would like to thank you for your interest in the Herald Charitable Foundation. We would also like to thank you for the time you took in completing our funding application. We enjoyed learning about your organization.*

*As you may know, the competition for funding is large. While we value the work that your organization does and consider your needs to be well within our priorities, we regret to inform you that your request for funding has been denied.*

*Though we have chosen not to fund your organization during this funding cycle, we ask that you stay in touch with our staff and keep us apprised of your activities. Again, we enjoyed reading and learning about your organization, and we look forward to hearing from you in the future.*

*Sincerely,*
*The Herald Charitable Foundation*

With this letter, Rose has another kind of stewardship task at hand. Rose may feel disappointed that her request for funding was denied. She may feel that she spent a great deal of time putting the grant proposal together — only to be rejected. In times like this, your first inclination may be to crumble the rejection letter into a ball and pitch it into the garbage, but do not feel vastly disappointed. The letter sent by the Herald Charitable Foundation did hold out promise of a future relationship and stated that the foundation considers Amicitia Community Gardens' needs to be well within the foundation's priorities for funding.

Sometimes you have to be prepared to knock on a door more than once before someone answers. For Rose and Amicitia Community Gardens, this is one of those times. Rose now has to figure out a strategy to keep the Herald Charitable Foundation up-to-date on the activities of Amicitia Community Gardens. She feels that it is important that she treat them the same way she treats the Westview Community Foundation, in many respects. She adds the Herald Charitable Foundation to Amicitia Community Gardens' mailing list. She notes that they should be invited to all garden openings. Finally, she writes a letter to the foundation to invite a foundation representative on a tour of a community garden.

Rose then refers back to her grants calendar and makes a note of the next funding cycle that Amicitia Community Gardens may again make a proposal to the Herald Charitable Foundation. She plans on knocking on their door again. Next time, however, the foundation will have more knowledge of Amicitia Community Gardens and its programs.

Rose's reaction to the rejection letter she received from the Herald Charitable Foundation may have been different if the letter stated that they did not fund community gardens or if Amicitia Community Gardens' activities did not fall in line with foundation priorities. At that point, Rose would have to determine whether it was worth her time, energy, and money to keep the foundation up-to-date with Amicitia Community Gardens' activities.

Because Rose sees her job as Executive Director of Amicitia Community Gardens as chief friend-maker as well as chief grant-seeker, she understands the need to attract potential stakeholders. Even though the Herald Charitable Foundation did not fund her organization, she feels that she succeeded in creating a new relationship. Likewise, she feels that she was successful in bringing the Westview Community Foundation into the center of the Amicitia Community Gardens stakeholders. Now, stewardship of both new relations is important as Amicitia Community Gardens works to keep the community foundation at the center of the circle and continues to move the Herald Charitable Foundation toward the center.

Other reasons the grant proposal could be denied might include:

- Not enough information about the organization
- Incomplete application
- Views of project did not correspond with the views of the foundation
- Grant proposal was not received by deadline
- Amount requested was not in line with foundation giving abilities
- Organization submitting the proposal is outside the foundation's geographic giving area
- There were inconsistencies in the proposal narrative and budget

If your grant proposal is denied for any of these reasons, you should re-evaluate your grant proposal and foundation research. If the foundation is not specific as to why they have denied your proposal, ask them to explain the denial further so you can improve your proposal. Most organizations will give you a reason for funding denial. Take this as constructive criticism, and use it to strengthen your proposal.

You may be able to reapply at a later time to a foundation that denied funding, if your missions are similar. If you are unable to reapply to a foundation, look for other foundations with the same mission and vision as your organization. Now that you know what to improve on, you will have a better chance of being awarded funding next time.

# Chapter 23

## Partial Funding and Project Changes

We have learned the fate of two of the grant proposals that Rose sent off. You may be wondering what happened to the grant proposal she sent off to the XYZ Foundation. As you recall, this proposal was a request for $45,000 to hire and train nine associate gardeners over the next three years. In this situation the proposal was awarded funding, but it was not for the full amount requested.

In many instances in life, there are circumstances presented to us that we have to work around. The same is true for grant seeking. In this chapter we will explore this situation of partial funding and also if:

- The project that was funded does not occur
- The funded project fails
- When planned projects do not receive funding

Sometimes, the toughest decision you have to make in handling funding decisions is how to deal with partially funded projects. When projects are fully funded, you fly into them with the satisfaction of knowing that all the financial support you need is there to help you on your way to a successful program. When a project is not funded at all, while that is disappointing, it is not difficult to make the decision to postpone the project until the funding issue is settled. We will read more about that decision-making process a little later in this chapter. But, what do you do when you get a letter like the one Rose received from the XYZ Foundation?

## Sample Funding Announcement Letter

*XYZ Charitable Foundation*
*Mr. Samuel Zander Jr., President*
*Box 432*
*Blanton, IN 44444*

*Rose Flowers*
*Executive Director*
*Amicitia Community Gardens*

*Dear Ms. Flowers:*

*Thank you for submitting your proposal for funding to the XYZ Charitable Foundation. It is my great pleasure to inform you that you have been awarded a foundation grant in the amount of $25,000 for the proposed project you submitted to our foundation.*

*We realize that the awarded amount is less than the amount requested. We are certain, however, that the amount awarded will not hinder your plans to engage in the project as planned.*

*Enclosed with this letter is a copy of your original proposal and an award agreement that is to be signed and returned to our office within 30 days. If you have any questions about any of the enclosed documents, please do not hesitate in contacting us.*

*Again, we thank you for your proposal. We are looking forward to working with Amicitia Community Gardens as partners to make the city of Westview a green and growing community.*

*Sincerely,*
*Samuel Zander, Jr., President*
*XYZ Charitable Foundation*

While Rose was quite excited to receive this letter and the award it announced, she knew that she had to think about her organization's plans and their ability to enter into the project before it was fully funded. She needed to consider her options. She could do any of the following:

- Accept the money and scale back the program
- Turn the funding down and scrap the program
- Accept the funding and look for a way to fund the rest of the program
- Accept the funding and make the program work with less money
- Do a combination of the above options

There was no mention in the letter Rose received from the XYZ Foundation about submitting plans for this change in funding — that is, what Amicitia Community Gardens might plan to do with less money than they had initially asked for. However, if you submit a proposal to a foundation and are awarded only a portion of the proposed amount, you may be required to resubmit your plans with adjustments.

The project Rose was trying to fund through this grant was a multiyear project that proposed hiring nine Amicitia Community Garden associate gardeners over a three-year period. The funding being awarded by the XYZ Foundation was a bit more than half of what the original proposed budget called for. In terms of the cycle of this specific grant, Rose believed she had the time and the support to enter into the project as planned and continue her fund-raising efforts to fund the project as it was originally outlined.

The way she saw it, the associate gardeners were to be hired to support the growth of the organization as they established more gardens in more neighborhoods. The grant they were to receive from the Westview Community Foundation assured their growth in respect to the number of gardens and stakeholders. Rose felt certain that this growth would enable them to continue the associate gardener project, though the road to the completion of this objective was not as straight as it may have been if the project were fully funded by the XYZ Foundation. The changes brought about by the funding awarded by the XYZ Foundation would come about in Rose's development plans and in her annual organizational plans.

It might not have been as easy for Rose to decide what to do in the above circumstance if the XYZ Foundation had granted Amicitia Community Gardens only $5,000. In such a case, Rose might consider seriously paring back the project. A grant of $5,000 would allow her to hire and train only one associate gardener. While one is better than nothing, she was certain that as more gardens were established as a result of the grant from the Westview Community Foundation, she would require more help. She could accept the funding and change the job description of the associate gardener, making it a position that is primarily concerned with volunteer development and training, but that sounds like a full-time position. A grant of $5,000 will not pay for a full-time employee. She might consider turning the funding down because she could not see how to proceed with the project without adequate funding.

## Grant $eeking Tip

If you are offered a lesser grant than you requested, there are a number of factors that you must take into account. You need to consider your organization's ability to carry out the project with less money. If you cannot see how the project can proceed, you need to turn the funding down. It is a difficult choice to make, but if you honestly cannot make the project work, it is better to politely turn the funding down with an explanation regarding the reality of the situation. Continue in your stewardship of your relationship with the foundation, and try again another time.

Think about what might happen if you accept the funding and the project fails due to insufficient funds. You will find yourself writing a final report describing a failed program that you might have suspected to fail from the beginning.

Let us look at a similar issue from another perspective. Think about a situation in which a project is funded and then does not take place. For instance, if Amicitia Community Gardens had received funding for associate gardeners from the XYZ Foundation, and after three years, no associate gardeners had been hired or trained. This example is a bit of a stretch in that the project was a multi-year project that probably required annual reporting, but it will suffice as an example.

## What Happens When the Proposed Project Does Not Take Place

There are countless reasons why projects do not take place, and they each fall into one of two categories — the unavoidable and the avoidable. We will just say that after three years, Amicitia Community Gardens did not hire any associate gardeners. Now it is time to write a final report. What do you do? Was the reason that no gardeners were hired unavoidable? Did a tornado wipe out all of Amicitia Community Gardens' gardens and change their priorities? This is unavoidable. Or, did Rose just put off hiring people (for whatever reason), and the project just never happened? This is avoidable. An act of bad administration is not a good excuse.

Whatever happened to put you in a situation in which the project did not occur, spell out the facts truthfully. The fact is, if the project did not happen due to bad organizational administration, you may not get funding from the foundation again in the near future, or ever. If the project did not occur because of an unavoidable situation, be honest about it. You may have another chance at funding from the foundation in the future.

In either case, you will likely have to return the grant. This goes back to stewardship. Do not spend the grant money on anything other than what it was intended for. In many cases if you, for any reason, do not carry out the proposed project, you will need to be able to return the money awarded. You will sign an agreement as you enter into a grant, and it is vital that you comply with the agreement you sign.

## What Happens if the Proposed Project Does not Meet the Objective

A failed project is quite a different scenario than a project that does not occur. True, a project that does not occur is a failed project, but sometimes things do not always go as planned.

Let us suppose that Amicitia Community Gardens' quest to establish a community garden in every precinct of Westview was nearing the end of its grant cycle. Amicitia Community Gardens received a capacity-building grant from the Westview Community Foundation for $60,000. The grant proposal stated that the capacity-building project that would occur was the establishment of nine community gardens, which would give Amicitia Community Gardens a garden in every precinct of Westview. At the end of the first year, they had established only one garden. Three gardens were started in the second year, and one was established in the third and final year of the grant cycle. At the end of three years, Amicitia Community Gardens had established five gardens of the proposed nine.

Amicitia Community Gardens did not meet their planned objective. Compare this final report with the final report in the last chapter. They are both reports from the same project. The last chapter shows the report from a project that was highly successful. The following report indicates that an unforeseen problem caused them to change their plans and, even then, they did not meet their proposed objectives.

# Grantee Report Narrative

Please review and include your original grant proposal and grant agreement.

**State the purpose of the grant. Please include a statement about the population served during the grant period.**

*The grant awarded to Amicitia Community Gardens by the Westview Community Foundation was a capacity-building project that had been outlined in and a primary objective of Amicitia Community Gardens' long-term strategic plan. The primary organizational goal was to further develop the Community Garden Initiative. Toward that goal, the proposed project was to establish at least one community garden in each precinct of the city in a three-year time period.*

*The population that was most directly served was the community of gardeners that live in the city precincts where the new gardens were established. The students that attend Westview Public Schools in the neighborhoods where these new gardens were planted were also served. Indirectly served was the commu-*

*nity-at-large, as these gardens were located in neighborhood lots that were designated as blighted.*

**Describe the activities the organization engaged in to accomplish the objectives identified in the grant proposal.**

*The fulfillment of this capacity-building initiative called upon Amicitia Community Gardens to establish nine community gardens in nine precincts of the city over the three-year period.*

*To accomplish our objective, Amicitia Community Gardens secured land on which to establish the gardens, made tools and sundry gardening necessities (seed, soil, fertilizer, and etcetera) available for gardeners, recruited and trained volunteer gardeners, and hired and trained gardening associates.*

*Amicitia Community Gardens established one new garden in the third precinct in the first year of the initiative. Gardens were planted in the seventh, eighth, and ninth precincts in the following spring. One garden was established in the fifth precinct this past spring.*

**To what extent were the intended activities accomplished?**

*We had intended to establish nine community gardens over a three-year period in city precincts where there were no community gardens. At the project's end, there would be a community garden in every precinct of Westview. At the end of the three-year period, Amicitia Community Gardens established five community gardens. While we have not reached our nine-garden objective, which would have given the city a community garden in each of its precincts, we do feel that we have grown the capacity of our organization.*

**Briefly describe any collaborative efforts or partnerships involved in planning or implementing this project.**

*Amicitia Community Gardens has an excellent working relationship with the City of Westview and has been fortunate that the city places a high value on the work that Amicitia Community Gardens is doing. The city has been, and continues to be, a valuable partner as they worked with us to identify compatible locations in city neighborhoods. These locations not only include garden spots, but locations for potential farmers' markets, as well.*

*Amicitia Community Gardens also considers all the neighborhood gardeners that have worked so hard with us to establish all of our gardens as valuable partners. Without the collaboration of the people in each precinct of Westview, our work would have proved untenable.*

**Briefly describe the expected outcomes of the project.**

*As Amicitia Community Gardens had proposed a capacity-building initiative that called upon the organization to establish community gardens, we have had to assess the project on two different levels.*

*To achieve our objectives and build capacity, we expected to establish a community garden in each precinct of the city. This objective was not met.*

*Primarily, we have had to assess the capacity building focus of our project. Though we have not yet established the number of gardens that we had proposed, we do feel that we have grown the capacity of our organization. We have established five new gardens in Westview, increased the number of organizational stakeholders, and developed new parameters for identifying land suitable for community gardens. We feel that this project has had a positive impact of the growth and long-term goals of our organization.*

**Briefly describe the extent to which these expected outcomes have been realized.**

*Growth has come as we have increased the number of gardens and stakeholders involved in our organization. We have seen growth in funding from earned and unearned revenue sources.*

**Briefly describe the unexpected outcomes (positive or negative) that resulted from the project.**

*We did not expect the issue of land suitability to be as big of an issue as it was in identifying garden locations. Several locations that had been identified by the city as suitable for community gardens were found to be not suitable due to the existence of soil contamination. These identified plots were in areas of the city with a high concentration of industry. We are still searching for garden locations in these precincts, but the cost of cleaning up the soil in some locations is currently beyond our means.*

*Amicitia Community Gardens has had an unexpected growth in interest from "backyard" gardeners from all over the city as a result of our increased visibility. We are in the process of enhancing our ability to assist these gardeners, as they have always been a part of our vision. However, we were not prepared for the number of these gardeners that have approached us for assistance in a variety of different ways. Thus, this unexpected growth has been both a positive outcome and a negative one.*

**Briefly describe the strengths and weaknesses of the project. Please detail how your organization addressed project weaknesses.**

*The primary weakness of the project is that, from the beginning, it was tied closely to another grant-funded initiative. This, though it could have been a strength, proved to be a weakness in that the project was only partially funded. The funding was to be for associate gardeners that were to work part-time in the new community gardens.*

*The organization's staff turned to our vast volunteer base for support, which was one of our strengths. A volunteer call was put out to enlist a group of specialized volunteer gardeners that have the knowledge and experience necessary to serve temporary posts as volunteer associate gardeners.*

*Another weakness, one we did not foresee prior to entering into this project, was our ability to deal with land deemed unsuitable for gardening due to contamination. We are currently working with stakeholders and other interested parties to come up with a plan that would help communities clean up contaminated soil in their yards and neighborhoods.*

**Please identify changes that were made in the project plan.**

*As we encountered problems in identifying land suitable to garden on, we scaled back our expectations regarding garden numbers in the third year of this project. By the end of year two, we had established four gardens and determined that, rather than aim at establishing nine gardens over three years; we would set our goal at seven. This number was realized, as we have now established five new gardens over this three-year period.*

**Briefly describe your plan for project sustainability.**

*Amicitia Community Gardens has been working diligently to construct a many-tiered, dynamic development mechanism. We continuously work to expand our circle of stakeholders who work and act as volunteers, contributors, and supporters of our mission. We, our organization and community gardeners, have begun several commercial ventures that will assist in supporting not only our gardeners, but our organization as well. Through our growing farmers' markets and our increasing relationships with restaurants in the city, we are seeing an increase in our earned income. Our growing reputation as a well-grounded community organization that is true to our mission with a clear vision is gen-*

*erating a great deal of interest from the funding community. This interest is helping us to see growth in our unearned income.*

*Besides the financial support we have seen from individual donors and from charitable foundations such as the Westview Community Foundation, we have noted a large increase in in-kind support over the past three years. Home Supply Stores, Vantage Superstores, and Westview Home Improvement have all been valuable in-kind contributors to our community gardens.*

*Our continued growth and efforts to build a support network have been extremely fruitful, and we expect our gardens to continue to flourish well into the future.*

While the report describes a project that was probably extremely disappointing for Amicitia Community Gardens, it also describes an organization that learned some valuable lessons. While Amicitia Community Gardens failed to establish nine community gardens in the three-year project period, they did succeed in building capacity, and they learned some tough lessons about soil contamination that they may be able to use to help their community.

The lesson we can take from this final report is that it is possible to turn what might seem like a failure on the surface into a positive organizational experience. Amicitia Community Gardens worked hard and was a responsible steward of the money awarded to them by the Westview Community Foundation. When it came time to write the final grant report, they spoke plainly and clearly about the problems that arose. They did what was expected of them.

What might have happened to this gardening initiative if they had not received any funding? The expansion of community gardens across the city was a primary objective of the organization. It might appear that without funding, the project may not have gone forward.

Ultimately, raising funds is likely not the mission of your organization. True, the funding can often help to support the mission, but it is vital that you understand the need to develop a successful multi-tiered development plan.

The tiers of this development plan are only bound by your imagination and may include partnerships, memberships, stakeholders, earned income initiatives, and a variety of unearned income strategies. The more diverse your development strategies are, the more successful your foundation grant search will be — and the more successful your organization will be. If you can show that you have a solid base of individual donors, government support, and business sponsors from your community — and have creatively developed your earned-income strategy — foundations feel comfortable knowing that you will handle the money they award you responsibly.

This chapter explores the many situations that can occur during the foundation funding process. Sometimes things are better than expected, and sometimes they are worse than expected. Sometimes things are just different. Be flexible. Be prepared for change. Have a "Plan B" and a "Plan C." The more prepared you are from the outset, the easier it will be to operate.

# Chapter 24

## Sound Advice

The case studies presented throughout this book offer advice for researching, preparing for, and writing foundation grants. Go beyond these short case studies and talk to those who have been there before you. As you speak with grant writers, development directors, and executive directors of non-profits, take note of their trials as well as their triumphs. Talk to them about what makes proposals successful. You will, most likely, hear many of the same things that you have read in the case studies. You will hear about partnerships and personal relationships as you seek to increase your stakeholders.

Your partners and stakeholders can offer you important advice. Seek their counsel:

- When you come across a weak area in your strategic plan. If you are an organization that has examined strengths and weaknesses as part of your strategic planning process, you might consider partners that can help you in your weak areas.

- When in need of a new ideas. Stakeholders are a wonderful source of collaboration, and they can offer a different perspective.

- When you are faced with a problem. Explore those that have a stake in the problem you are looking to solve. Amicitia Community Gardens considered the city government of Westview to be a valuable partner as they worked to rid the city of blighted city lots.

If you are an individual looking for funding for a project, you might consider looking to umbrella organizations as partners. These are organizations whose mission is to assist individuals and small organizations — usually start-ups — with the business and support of their mission. The Kodiak Arts Council, the case study featured at the end of this chapter, is an umbrella organization. One of the services they provide their members is their not-for-profit status — their 501(c) (3) status — to assist in raising funds. This type of two-way collaboration allows individuals and small organizations to raise foundation funds and allows the Kodiak Arts Council the opportunity to pursue its mission of promoting and supporting the arts.

Go into grant-seeking knowing that most proposals are not funded. Do not let that deter you. Raising money, whether through foundation grants or individual appeals, is a numbers game. The more doors you knock on, the greater chance there is that you will succeed. Of course, you have to be knocking on the right doors. Knowing the right avenues to take during your pursuit for funding is vital; do your research to find the best places in your community to contact.

Your proposal is the first impression a foundation gets from you. It is important that you work through this process carefully to avoid any mistakes and strengthen your proposal. Here is a list of ten things you can do to strengthen your proposal's chances of being accepted:

1. Make sure that you have researched a foundation carefully before you submit a proposal so you meet the foundation's priorities.

2. Read and thoroughly understand the foundation's guidelines before beginning your proposal.

3. Read and thoroughly understand the foundation's application before beginning your proposal.

4. To assure that your proposal is well-written and clear, have an individual whom you trust read and critique it before submittal.

5. Keep your funding request within the funding range of the identified foundation.

6. Do everything you can to establish a relationship with the foundation before you submit a proposal.

7. Make sure that the need your proposal addresses is one that goes beyond your organization and into the community.

8. Do everything you can to assure that your proposed project is **SMART: S**pecific, **M**easurable, **A**chievable, **R**ealistic, and **T**imely.

9. Provide proof that the proposed project is sustainable after the proposed grant cycle.

10. Remember that the grant is not about you, but the mission of your organization. If you are rejected for funding, do not take it personally. Try it again the next opportunity you get.

Seeking grants from foundations is an extremely competitive endeavor. As such, it is vital that you are meticulous in your presentation. Double-check your:

- Spelling
- Grammar
- Math
- Attachments
- Signatures
- Addresses

It is important to give yourself time to review your proposal and to make any revisions. Allow sufficient time for this process, and do not rush your proposal out the door.

## CASE STUDY: NANCY KEMP, EXECUTIVE DIRECTOR

Executive Director
Kodiak Arts Council
P.O. Box 1792
Kodiak, AK 99615
**www.kodiakartscouncil.org**

The Kodiak Arts Council was incorporated as Kodiak Baranof Productions in December 1963 and is now doing business as Kodiak Arts Council.

The Kodiak Arts Council is a local arts agency that presents a performing arts series each year and offers a summer arts camp for children. It is an umbrella organization to 15 local arts groups that works through the Kennedy Center Partners in Education program with the Kodiak Island Borough School District to integrate the arts into the school curriculum.

I have been writing foundation grants for seven years. I search for capital-improvements funding. We also seek funding for new technology equipment, software, and improvements to our community's auditorium (e.g., new lighting equipment, sound equipment, and replacement of all of the curtains).

The amount we receive varies from year to year. In my ten years, we received four foundation grants totaling approximately $100,000. My predecessor garnered approximately ten foundation grants in 18 years.

I believe funders find the Kodiak Arts Council attractive because we have been in business successfully for 46 years; we are flexible with change and stable with our local support.

As a grant seeker, I look for a funder that matches our need(s) and one whose restrictions we can match. I think a compelling grant proposal is one that honestly and clearly states a need that is in line with a grantor's objectives.

In my humble opinion, I would say, in seeking foundation funding, put time in on developing a personal relationship with the foundation's representative. This can be accomplished through e-mail and phone conversations, asking pertinent questions so the grant application follows the foundation's funding rules and intentions.

# Conclusion

Nobody said writing a foundation grant proposal was going to be easy. There is considerable preparation involved. However, once you are prepared, it is not as hard as it seems. Grant writing is a skill. Being able to engage in grant writing takes practice. The process of preparing, researching, writing, editing, submitting, and tracking foundations takes considerable time and energy. Take your time. Prepare methodically.

If you are new to the grant-seeking world, following the steps set forth in this book will set you on the right path.

1. Compose a clear and concise mission statement
2. Elucidate an ideal vision
3. Work with stakeholders to construct a measurable long-term strategic plan
4. Ensure your financial records are kept up-to-date and in order
5. Work with stakeholders to know and prioritize your organizational needs
6. Do your research and know the funding community

7. Organize your search
8. Stick to deadlines
9. Recognize and thank your stakeholders
10. Try again, if at first you do not succeed

The most important thing to remember about writing grants is that grant writing is a tool to help you achieve your goals. Whether you are a professional grant writer or volunteer writing grants for a local nonprofit, the mission and vision of that organization must be your highest priority.

To act according to the mission of your organization you should remember that, for the long-term health of your organization, you must prepare to deal with the ebbs and flows of any of your funding lines. The world of foundation grants and their funding priorities often change as our world and economy changes.

In the same manner that you construct a many-tiered development plan, you must also build a diverse network of foundation, corporate, and government granting relationships. Building, fostering, and guiding these relationships should be pursued in a most organized, conscientious manner.

Good luck in your quest, and be prepared to experience the thrill of acceptance.

# Appendix

## Frequently Asked Questions

Some of the most frequently asked questions grant writers ask are presented here as a resource. These answers should help you better understand the entire money-gathering process and how to best meet the needs of the foundations while getting the funds you need.

### 1. How do I know if I am even eligible for a grant?

*Grants are increasingly gaining popularity with organizations and individuals. The truth remains: Not every person or organization is eligible for grant money. First and foremost, most foundations require that you have a 501(c) (3) standing with the IRS that formally acknowledges your non-profit status. If you do not have this status, your road to foundation grant funding is more challenging, though not impossible. Even having non-profit status does not guarantee you any money. To see whether you qualify for a grant from a specific agency or foundation, check their guidelines and requirements carefully. They will clearly state who is eligible for grant awards and who is not. In the resource section* of this book that follows this FAQ, you will find a Web site called Foundation Grants to Individuals Online. This will give you some direction.

## 2. Are grant makers willing to talk with grant seekers?

If you are new at the grant game, you may be hesitant to take weeks to write a funding proposal without first talking with someone at the foundation about what they want. Some foundations are more than willing to answer a few of your basic questions. Some will walk you through the entire process; others have neither the time nor the staff to do more than read what you send. To determine which is which, pick up the phone and ask. You have nothing to lose and much valuable information to gain from simply asking for help.

## 3. I have a creative way of presenting my organization's need. Can I do it and bypass the foundation's normal guidelines?

Do so at your own risk. Foundations have certain submission guidelines for a reason and may require that all submissions follow them. While it is not unheard of to try something new and different to grab some attention for your proposal, it is not advisable. Instead, try to find a creative way to submit your proposal without offending the foundation by ignoring their rules. On the other hand, the world of philanthropic giving is changing pretty radically. Many foundations determine who they award money to based on many things other than a formal application. This gets back to relationship building. So, before you work up that interpretive dance grant proposal, talk to the foundation to find out what is acceptable.

**4. If I have done a good job of presenting my need, do I need to include all the extra documents in the appendices?**

*Yes. All of those extra documents are needed to set your proposal apart from other, less informative proposals. Sure, they can be a pain to gather, sort, and include — but they are necessary.*

**5. What are some of the biggest pet peeves that grant makers have?**

*There are many things that frustrate grant makers these days, but here is a list of their top annoyances:*

- *Grant seekers who never research the foundation and the types of programs they support*
- *Grant seekers who present no needs statement*
- *Grant seekers who present no plan for assessing their projects*
- *Grant seekers who present no plan for program/project sustainability*
- *Incomplete proposals that are submitted with little thought or planning*
- *Grant seekers requesting funding beyond the funding range of the foundation*
- *Grant seekers who have no idea how much a project is going to cost*
- *Grant seekers who assume that their program is the only one the grant maker may be considering and do not understand why they may be denied funding*
- *Grammatical and spelling mistakes*
- *Inconsistencies throughout the proposal*

**6. What do I do if a foundation does not have application guidelines?**

*At one time, this was quite unusual, but it is becoming increasingly common. Some foundations do allow grant seekers to submit proposals in any form or style they wish, even over lunch or a round of golf. In any case, you should be* prepared with the same kind of information that you would have in preparing a written proposal. You may want to have a written proposal that follows your oral presentation, and you should always be prepared with your mission/vision/needs statement. Know how much your project is going to cost, and have an assessment strategy. Whether you pitch your project over coffee or as a formal proposal, the deliverables are, for the most part, the same.

## 7. How do I find out whether my proposal is being considered?

No news may seem like good news, but not in the grant-writing world. Failure to hear from a grant maker within 90 days of their meeting usually means that your proposal has been denied outright. Check the foundation guidelines again to see what they might say about their decision-making process and schedule. Some foundations send standard rejection letters or postcards; others do not. If you are concerned that your request has even arrived, feel free to make a brief call of inquiry. But be prepared to hear the old adage: "If we're interested, we will contact you." After 60-90 days, it is acceptable to assume that your request has been denied; move on to another foundation or funding strategy for help.

## 8. How long does it take to get funding?

Applying for and receiving grant money takes time — anywhere from a month or two to a year or more. The average time is about 12-18 months. It often takes 30-90 days to hear from a foundation after sending a letter of inquiry. Once an application packet arrives, it can take one to three months to write your full proposal, and another three months or more to hear whether it has been approved. Once approved, it can take another month or more to receive the much-anticipated check. That means it can take about one full year from the time you first contact a funder until you have a check in hand. Again, it all depends on the foundation and the relationship you have with them.

## 9. When should we consider calling it quits?

*Being a rejected a few times is no reason to consider dropping a program you feel passionate about. However, if a funder denies your request, giving you roughly the same reasons you have heard before — the request is too expensive, or that you are not prepared to handle a project this size — then you may want to reconsider whether your project is possible. Remember, though, it is not about the fundraising; it is about your mission.*

## 10. Do we have to use the grant money received for the items listed in our proposal? What if new needs arise?

*You will sign, or have signed, a funding agreement. You are required by law to use the funds awarded as outlined in your proposal and funding agreement — with little or no exception. Should new needs arise, feel free to contact your funder and ask permission to shift some monies toward them, but be prepared to hear "no." Many foundations will require you to submit an entirely new application for changing funds even slightly, which could result in your grant award being withdrawn.*

# Example Grant Proposals

## I. GRANT PROPOSAL

### REQUEST

*Youth Services Organization (YSO)[1] respectfully requests a grant of $100,000 from the Community Charitable Foundation, payable over a period of three to five years, toward the construction of a new children's crisis center.*

---

[1]The name of the organization, foundation, and some other names have been changed in this sample proposal.

*This new center will be built as a two-story addition on the south side of the Home for Children, located on South Boulevard. It will provide space for overnight emergency shelter for children ages birth to 18, family visitation, therapy, counseling, and the YSO foster care program.*

*This grant will allow YSO to (1) increase its emergency shelter capacity from 16 to 30 children and youth per day and (2) make important quality improvements to the way it provides shelter and services for children who have been removed from their homes and caregivers because of abuse or neglect.*

## PROJECT DESCRIPTION

*YSO operates the only emergency shelter for children in southeast Nebraska, providing abused, neglected, and homeless children with basic necessities and supportive services that help them recover from trauma and receive appropriate medical care, mental health treatment, and other services needed to help them find a permanent home and family.*

*YSO has been providing overnight shelter to children since 1947. The original YSO Home was constructed in 1953 and is still used today. The current facility reflects the orphanage-style care of a previous era when orphanage-style congregate living facilities were viewed as a long-term arrangement for abused or abandoned children. Rooms and offices are located off one long central hallway, with very limited space for programs that support a child's search for a permanent home and family.*

*Today's philosophy of care for children places a much greater emphasis on accurate and comprehensive assessments for each child; therapeutic healing from trauma; establishment of long-term foster care and/or adoptive families as soon as possible to provide the child with a sense of security and permanency; and family reunification whenever it is safe and possible. Congregate living is no longer considered a long-term solution. Rather, emergency shelter provides a place for children to be comforted, to have immediate basic needs met, for crisis intervention, stabilization, assessment, and for planning for the next and hopefully permanent placement.*[2]

*This two-story, 17,000-square-foot addition will allow YSO to collocate under one roof its foster care program, two emergency shelter programs (one for younger children and sibling groups; another for teenagers), family visitation, case management, counseling, and therapy.*

*The ground floor will be devoted to emergency shelter and assessment of younger children, ages 0-13, and sibling groups that include young children. These children will be accommodated in two apartment-style living areas, each with two bedrooms adjacent to a central living room, plus a shared kitchen. This space will accommodate up to six children each night and will meet licensing requirements to house more children if necessary.*

*When not in use as an overnight shelter, these living areas will host family visitations, allowing children at YSO to visit with their family of origin and with prospective foster care families 'on their own turf.' Currently, children have to travel to YSO family visitation sites, which are located throughout the city. Providing family visitation at the shelter site will be a dramatic improvement for the children, supporting a sense of their own stability, comfort, and control. It also provides a way for the case management team, also located on-site, to supervise and assess family function in a home-like setting.*

*The ground floor of the new children's crisis center will also include a secure entrance and reception area, office space for case management, a large conference room area for foster family trainings, a family meeting room, and a therapy room.*

---

[2]Oakes, Emily Joyce and Madelyn Freundlich. The Role of Emergency Care as a Child Welfare Service. Child Welfare League of America, 2005, page 4.

*Emergency shelter for abused, neglected, homeless and runaway teens will be provided on the second level of the new addition. It will include six bedrooms for girls and six for boys; two gender-specific living areas with couches, tables, and study carrels; and a central shared commons area for group activities. The sleeping rooms will be used as single-capacity whenever possible, with the option to use them as double-capacity when necessary, serving up to 24 youth. Case management, therapy, and counseling offices will be located on the second level, plus an activity area for staff-led group activities, team meetings, and training sessions. This new space will provide improved staff oversight for everyone's safety and improved living conditions for the teens.*

## NEED FOR THE PROJECT

*Nebraska, and Blank County in particular, has a recognized need to improve services to abused, neglected, and homeless children.*

*In 2006, Blank County had the highest substantiated rate of abuse/neglect of all Nebraskan counties: 17.8 abused and neglected children per 10,000, for a total of 1,343 cases.*

*Nebraska ranks first in the nation, per capita, in the number of children living in out-of-home placements due to abuse or neglect. According to the Nebraska Foster Care Review Board's 2006 Annual Report, "Each day, an average of 13 Nebraska children and youth are removed from their home of origin, primarily due to abuse or neglect (4,768 children were removed in 2006)."[3]*

*Child abuse has been called the No. 1 public health crisis because of its potential for lasting and harmful repercussions. According to the Nebraska Foster Care Review Board's 2006 Annual Report, abused and neglected children:*

---

[3]Oakes, Emily Joyce and Madelyn Freundlich. The Role of Emergency Care as a Child Welfare Service. Child Welfare League of America, 2005, page 4.

- *Are often in special education*
- *Have increased likelihood of current/future drug and alcohol abuse*
- *Are more likely to have mental health needs*
- *Are more likely to be homeless*
- *Are more likely to enter the prison population*
- *May perpetuate the cycle of abuse as adults when they have children of their own[4]*

*Unfortunately, beyond the child's direct experiences of abuse or neglect, the experience of living in the child welfare system can often have negative repercussions as well.*

*In Nebraska, 55 percent of children in foster care have moved to a new home at least four times; 36 percent of children have experienced six or more placements in their lifetimes.[5] For children who are also coping with the trauma of abuse or neglect, these multiple placements can have profound and lasting implications on physical and mental health, and on normal childhood development. Several studies have indicated that instability in placements and multiple broken attachments to caregivers can:*

- *Hinder brain development in preschool-age children*
- *Predict high mental health service use*
- *Lead to exaggerated behavior problems, regressive behaviors, mood swings, learning difficulties, sleep disruptions, and reliving of earlier trauma*

*Thus, instability becomes self-perpetuating, causing the behaviors that predict another unsuccessful placement.*

---

[4]Stitt., page 5.

[5]Stitt, page 50.

## THE CHILDREN SERVED

*A conservative estimate is that this project will serve approximately 500 children and youth annually, ages birth to 18, including those who have been removed from home and family of origin due to abuse or neglect; unaccompanied homeless and runaway youth; and children privately referred in an effort to prevent loss of parental custody.*

*Last year, YSO provided 382 children and youth with emergency shelter services, and served nearly 200 children through foster care services (including some who received both emergency shelter and foster care services.) Approximately two-thirds of these children are wards of the state; one-third are privately referred to prevent the loss of parental custody.*

*In Nebraska, physical neglect is the most frequently cited cause of a child's removal from home and family of origin, followed by parental substance abuse. Several studies have found that living in poverty is a predictor for involvement with the child welfare system.*

*This project also will serve youth who are runaway or homeless. Studies suggest that nearly half (46 percent) of homeless or runaway youth have been physically abused, and nearly 20 percent have been sexually abused by a family or household member. Studies also have indicated that children who are in foster care are more likely to become homeless, and at an earlier age and for a longer period of time. Incidents of depression, severe anxiety, poor health, low self-esteem, conduct disorder, and post-traumatic stress syndrome are very prevalent among homeless teens.[6] YSO's Street Outreach program seeks to connect homeless and runaway youth in the city to shelter and supportive services. Last year, Street Outreach served 359 youth.*

---

[6]"Homeless Youth," National Coalition for the Homeless, Fact Sheet #13, August 2007.

*Minority children and youth tend to be over-represented in Nebraska's child welfare system. Among children who have been removed from home, approximately 34 percent are considered to be a racial or ethnic minority, while only 15 percent of Nebraska's child population is considered minority.[7] Among those served by YSO, approximately 36 percent are from minority groups.*

## EFFECT OF THE PROJECT ON THE CHILDREN SERVED

*This project will:*

- *Allow YSO to update its orphanage-style shelter with a facility that will accommodate today's accepted best-practice methods for serving children who have been abused, neglected, or homeless*

- *Improve the resources available to care for children who have been removed from unsafe environments*

- *Increase YSO's emergency shelter capacity from 16 (current capacity) to 30*

- *Enable a new and innovative method of case management designed to reduce the negative effects of children living in the child welfare system*

- *Maximize the elements of child welfare services that have been shown to increase a child's likelihood of finding a permanent home and family*

---

[7]"KidsCount in Nebraska 2007 Report," Voices for Children in Nebraska, page 50.

*Those elements include:*

**Assessment**—*conducted in a natural environment where children can play, interact with others, and interact with family members, rather than as an isolated one-time interview*

**Family Visitation**—*where children, youth, and their family of origin or foster family can interact naturally and frequently in a home-like setting*

**Stable case management team**—*where one team of child-caring professionals remains focused on the child's needs, even as those needs change and evolve, until a successful, permanent placement is found.*

## Assessment

*YSO's emergency shelter plays a vital role in Blank County's child welfare system. Emergency shelter provides an appropriate and safe place for an accurate assessment completed by experienced staff. An accurate assessment is one of the child's best assurances that he or she will find an appropriate placement. For families, assessment of the child will help them understand and be prepared to cope with behaviors, expressions of grief, and other normal reactions to experiences of abuse, neglect, and removal from home. These "normal reactions" often include extreme emotions and disruptive behaviors. With ongoing family support, ongoing assessment that occurs during supervised family visitations, and visits from the case manager, families can receive information and guidance that helps them understand and appropriately engage with that child in ways that sustain the placement, rather than in ways that cause the placement to break down and become unsuccessful.*

## Family Visitation

*Family visitation is another key element in helping children find successful, long-term placements. One might assume that returning the child to his/her family of origin is the very last option. However, studies of children in foster care have shown that the child's best chance for securing a lasting and permanent home and family lies within that child's family of origin. According to Dr. Ann Coyne, University of Nebraska Omaha School of Social Work, "We all have a tendency to under-rate the risk to the child of being in the foster care system and over-rate the risk to the child of living in poverty in a dysfunctional family."[8] When the family of origin is not an immediate option, visitation with prospective foster families is essential for finding a successful foster placement for the child.[9]*

## Stable Case Management Team

*This new space and co-location of programs will allow YSO to adopt a new service delivery model, called Safe and Sound, which will significantly change the way it works with children. Currently, children are served in programmatic "silos" that, from the child's perspective, operate in relative isolation from each other. For example, when a child enters YSO emergency shelter, they are cared for and establish relationships with YSO shelter staff, including case managers and on-site caregivers. If that child moves to another YSO program, such as foster care, they are assigned a new team of program staff and caseworkers. They are required to retell their stories and re-establish trusting relationships with new staff members.*

*This can cause children to relive traumatic experiences, and changing caseworkers has been cited as one cause of children remaining in foster care longer, delaying a permanent placement for that child.[9]*

*YSO has been prevented from uniting these programmatic "silos" because space limitations have prohibited a necessary union of programs. In addition, about*

---

[8]Quoted in Stitt, page 30.

[9]Stitt, page 6.

*two-thirds of the children YSO serves are wards of the state. Complex and carefully designated state funding streams tied to specific children and specific services also have created barriers among programs. YSO is working with its governmental partners to reduce these barriers and serve state ward youth effectively, efficiently, and with transparency through this new case management concept.*

*In addition to the above benefits, this expansion will allow YSO to gain important operational efficiencies in staffing and in facility expense that will be an investment in the long-term financial health of the organization.*

## PARTNERSHIPS & COLLABORATIONS

*The emergency shelter services that YSO provides to unaccompanied children are unduplicated in southeast Nebraska. No other agency provides emergency shelter for children who have been removed from homes and caregivers.*

To complement its services to children and families, YSO has established many partnerships and service linkages for referrals, cooperation, and collaboration among agencies serving youth and families. For example:

- YSO has nurtured a strong working relationship with the County Youth Assessment Center and the Local Police Department to assist in locating and intervening with runaway youth and their families.

- With Friendship Home, the only domestic violence shelter in the city, and Voices of Hope (formerly known as the Rape/Spouse Abuse Crisis Center), YSO developed a standardized dating violence screening tool for use with runaway and homeless youth.

- YSO has maintained a relationship with Public Schools' Homeless Liaison for more than 15 years. The liaison identifies homeless youth and connects them to appropriate services. School achievement is one of the most important goals for youth at YSO, as so many have had negative school experiences and numerous school failures. This relationship allows these youth to have a positive school experience that may lead to greater investment in school and success in the future.

- YSO staff serve on committees and boards such as the Community Services Initiative, Runaway Response Team, Homeless Coalition, Outreach Alliance, Child Abuse Prevention Council, the Nebraska Association of Homes and Services Providers, and many more. Extensive networking enables YSO to make appropriate referrals of youth and families to a wide range of services.

## YSO ROOM TO GROW CAMPAIGN

*$2,000,000 of the new construction budget will be funded by contributions to the Room to Grow Campaign. The campaign is still in its early "quiet phase," soliciting leadership gifts and gifts from the YSO board of directors and foundation trustees. The campaign timeline is as follows:*

| Room to Grow Capital Campaign | October 2007 – September 2008 |
|---|---|
| Campaign Planning Phase | October – December 2007 |
| Quiet Phase, goal $1,000,000-$1,200,000 raised | January – May 2008 |
| Campaign Public Announcement | June 2008 |
| Public Phase, goal $800,000-$1,000,000 raised | June – September 2008 |

*As of April 18, 2008, the Room to Grow Campaign has raised $461,900 from 18 gifts.*

The YSO Room to Grow Campaign has recruited an excellent and committed leadership.

- *First Lady of Nebraska Jane Doe is serving as Honorary Chair. Her role in the campaign has been to help raise awareness of the needs among children who have been abused, neglected, or homeless, including the need for emergency shelter services. Her experiences as an educator have given her first-hand knowledge about the dire consequences of abuse and neglect in the lives of children. Her office as First Lady of Nebraska makes her an especially appropriate leader for an effort that will impact the lives of many state ward children.*

- *The campaign is being led by co-chairs John Smith, retired executive of Cornhusker Bank, and Sue Johnson, retired executive of MDS Pharma. Both are active in the community and have been involved with YSO for a combined three decades.*

Several attractive naming opportunities and donor recognition options have been developed. YSO would be pleased to discuss options for recognition of a gift from the Community Charitable Foundation.

## PROJECT BUDGET

| EXPENSES | |
|---|---|
| YSO children's crisis center wing | |
| General Construction | $2,650,500 |
| Site improvements, paving, parking | $153,062 |
| Signage | $7,500 |
| Contingency | $421,659 |
| Furnishings | $250,000 |
| Total | $3,482,721 |

| INCOME | |
| --- | --- |
| Room To Grow Campaign - $2,000,000 goal | |
| Confirmed gifts & pledges | $451,000 |
| Omaha Foundation request (pending) (1) | $500,000 |
| Children's Charitable Fund request (pending) | $200,000 |
| Community Charitable Foundation request | $100,000 |
| Community Health Foundation grant (planned) | $25,000 |
| Anticipated contributions | $724,000 |
| Subtotal | $2,000,000 |
| | |
| **FEDERAL APPROPRIATIONS (2)** | |
| 2007 Federal Appropriation (received) | $462,000 |
| 2008 Federal Appropriation (requested) (3) | $1,022,000 |
| Subtotal | $1,484,000 |
| | |
| *Grand Total* | *$3,484,000* |

(1) A proposal has been submitted to the Omaha Foundation requesting a $500,000 challenge grant. Notification is anticipated by June 30. A grant from the Community Charitable Foundation will count toward the match required by the Omaha Foundation, if awarded.

(2) This project has ramifications not only with child welfare services, but also with juvenile justice, homelessness, and the state-ward system. Because of this, it is uniquely qualified for federal appropriation funds from multiple sources. Last year, YSO, in partnership with Senator Morrison's office, was successful in securing federal support for the project through the Office of Juvenile Justice and Prevention and the Department of Housing and Urban Development. Congressman Ferry and Senator Morrison are both working to include the project in the current year's federal budget. Congressman Ferry's office has noti-

*fied YSO that the project is included in current draft of the House budget and that he will continue to advocate for the project. However, given the unpredictable nature of federal appropriations, YSO continues to seek other potential sources of support to secure the remaining project costs. YSO is considering a Community Development Block Grant and the Federal Home Loan Bank as additional possible sources of funding.*

*(3) YSO current federal appropriations request is $1,500,000. Approximately $1,022,000 of this year's request is for the construction of the children's crisis center. The remainder will be used to complete minor renovations to the existing YSO Home, including approximately $178,000 in renovations and approximately $300,000 to purchase and install a new HVAC system to replace the 1953 boiler system. These are the only renovations to be completed in the current home.*

## HISTORY & MISSION OF YSO

*YSO was founded in 1947 when _____ and _____ opened their home to abandoned and neglected children and youth. In 1953, the family purchased a farm on the Boulevard and constructed YSO Home for Children, the red brick building that is still used today to provide shelter and care for the city's abused, neglected and homeless children.*

*In 1996, YSO merged with Youth Service System and has continued to grow and expand to meet the needs of children and youth. In the past two years, YSO completed a strategic planning process that resulted in a more focused mission of helping children who have been abused, neglected, or homeless achieve safety, stability, and enduring family relationships. During 60 years of service, YSO has provided care and services for tens of thousands of children. Today, YSO has an annual operating budget of $12.5 million, which supports nearly 350 employees in 27 programs in this city, Hillstown, and West Forest. Last year,*

*YSO served more than 3,500 (unduplicated) children and youth and provided more than 67,000 nights of shelter.*

*YSO provides a wide range of services including emergency shelter, foster care, group residential care, residential mental health treatment, youth and family resiliency, and rural services, as well as early childhood development and school age programs for low-income families. YSO is licensed by the State of Nebraska as a Child Caring Agency, Child Placing Agency, and as a Child Care Center. The organization is an approved Medicaid and Medicaid Managed Care provider, and since 2001, YSO has received accreditation through the Council on Accreditation of Services for Children and Families (COA). In addition, YSO Early Childhood Development centers are accredited by the National Association for the Education of Young Children (NAEYC).*

*In 2005, YSO was awarded the first-ever Better Business Bureau Integrity Award in the nonprofit category.*

## ATTACHMENTS

- *Floor plans for the new addition*
- *Youth Services Organization Inc. IRS determination letter*
- *Youth Services Organization Inc. IRS Form 990*

## II. PROPOSAL NARRATIVE

## A. FUNDING REQUEST

### 1. Amount Requested

*TKF requests a grant for $5,000 from the A Foundation to help support a series of community strategic planning meetings to focus on creating community solutions to fight the epidemic of childhood obesity.*

## 2. Objective

TKF, a one-year-old organization, is planning a series of community forums to help it formulate a long-term strategic plan in support of its mission and vision. The TKF mission, in partnership with community members, is to prevent and reduce childhood obesity by empowering local children and families to eat healthy and be active. Our vision is to create community solutions to fight the epidemic of childhood obesity.

## 3. Population Served

According to the Robert Wood Johnson Foundation, we are raising the first generation of youth who will live sicker and die younger than their parents. In our own community, BMI data from local 5th-graders demonstrate significantly higher than national levels of obesity in children of lower socioeconomic status. Based on this and other data, our goals are to:

- Foster and facilitate partnerships among community organizations and members

- Lower obesity rates in local children

- Obtain measurable improvements in nutrition and physical activity in all local children

- Increase access to healthy foods and physical activity opportunities for all children and families

- Advocate for policy changes in support of these goals

- Ensure that children of all cultures and socioeconomic backgrounds are included in our mission

## 4. Effect

The objective of the community forums is to communicate organizational mission and vision to a community of stakeholders. The stakeholders, considering the epidemic proportion of the problem, are the community-at-large. It is also *our objective to get feedback from this community of stakeholders as to what they feel our roles should be in fighting this epidemic and what actionable objectives are necessary to achieve our stated goals.*

*The effect of the planned series of community forums on TKF is that the organization will have communicated its organizational mission and vision to the community-at-large and it will have gotten a good indication as to how the community feels we should attack this community health issue. We will better understand the history of the epidemic; where we currently stand regarding prevention and treatment of the problem; identify gaps in our community; measure outcomes; and determine where the need is greatest and where we will have the most impact.*

### 5. Partnerships

*TKF's identified working groups of stakeholders for the purpose of this series of planning forums are:*

- *Health care*
- *School systems,*
- *Childcare and preschool providers*
- *Governmental policies and programs*
- *Community-based organizations and faith groups*
- *Work sites, businesses, and restaurants.*

*To date, TKF has received grant funding from the Community Health Endowment to work on school policy reform and the NMA to start the Physicians for a Healthy Nebraska Obesity Prevention Project, which will include a policy clearinghouse. TKF has also received a grant from the Nebraska Department of Health and Human Services for the development of physician toolkits, a webinar, and office resources. We are also collaborating with the County Health Department on a social marketing cam-*

*paign that will be run through organizations, businesses, and schools in the North 27th neighborhoods.*

## 6. Work Plan

The schedule of the planned meetings is as follows:

*Kick-Off Event, Bryan/LGH—Tuesday, November 3, 2009 –The Kick-Off Event will introduce the community-at-large to the organization and its purpose. The event will serve as an informational gathering.*

*Health care stakeholders—Tuesday, November 10*

*Schools- Before/after school programs stakeholders—Tuesday, November 17*

*Childcare and preschool providers stakeholders—Tuesday, December 1*

*Governmental policies and programs stakeholders—Tuesday, December 8*

*Community-based organizations and faith groups—Tuesday, December 15*

*Work sites, businesses, and restaurants stakeholders—Tuesday, January 5, 2010*

*Teach a Kid to Fish Long-Term Plan Announcement—Wednesday, February 24, 2010*

## 7. Evaluation Plan

*Evaluation of this project will be an ongoing and dynamic process. As the outcome of the project will be a long-term strategic plan with measurable objectives, evaluation and planning updates will be built into the plan itself. Also, community stakeholders will be asked, as a follow-up procedure, to provide TKF with their thoughts and opinions regarding our planning process.*

_____, M.D., is a community pediatrician who left her practice to found and serve as executive director of TKF, a nonprofit organization working to prevent and reduce childhood obesity.

_____ is a family physician finishing his Master's in Public Health at Johns Hopkins, concentrating on health policy and child health and obesity. He is currently working schools to try and change/improve policies and track our child obesity & fitness rates.

_____, R.D., M.P.A., is the Assistant Director of the local County Medical Society. She serves on multiple state and local children's nutrition and physical activity committees, and is collaborating with TKF on several initiatives, including school policy reform.

_____ is a marketing communications specialist with more than 20 years of experience working in partnership development, community relations, and advertising. She was formerly the healthy lifestyles team leader for our nation's largest student organization.

## B. FINANCIAL PLAN

### 1. Project Budget

| Expenses | Cash | In-kind | |
|---|---|---|---|
| Administration | $1,000.00 | | |
| | | | |
| Facilities | | | |
| Kick-off Event | | $1,000.00 | Bryan/LGH |
| Stakeholder's Forums | $1,800.00 | | _____ |
| Hospitality | $5,000.00 | | |
| | | | |
| Communications | | | |
| Printing/Invitations | $125.00 | | ___ (Pending) |

| | | | |
|---|---|---|---|
| Mailing/Invitations | $275.00 | | ___ (Pending) |
| On-Site Information | $500.00 | | ___ (Pending) |
| | | | |
| **TOTAL EXPENSE** | **$9,700.00** | | |

### 3. Development Plan

*TKF is a relatively new organization that is in the process of talking and listening to the community as it develops its long-term strategic plan. Part of the plan will be a long-term plan of development that will serve the organizational mission. For this particular project, TKF has received support from Bryan/LGH and has a request pending from The American Medical Association.*

*TKF is certain that with a long-term strategic plan in place that includes actionable and measurable objectives, we will build a sustainable organization with the vision of creating community solutions to fight the epidemic of childhood obesity.*

### 4. Timing

*The funding for this project is needed September 1, 2009.*

## C. BACKGROUND OF THE ORGANIZATION

### 1. History & Mission

*TKF is a nonprofit organization founded in 2008 by _____ M.D., who left her practice to address the growing epidemic of poor nutrition and physical inactivity in our community's children. The childhood obesity epidemic has reached alarming levels. Multiple studies show increasing levels over the last thirty years, with a tripling of prevalence over that time period. At least one-third of our community's children are considered overweight or obese. Minority children, impoverished children, and children who live in certain neighborhoods without access to healthy foods and safe play spaces are disproportionately affected by the obesity epidemic. These populations have even high-*

er rates of diabetes, high blood pressure, and early heart disease. Obese children face a myriad of health, emotional, and social consequences as a result of this epidemic.

The childhood obesity epidemic is a public health emergency. Targeting children is a preventive measure to control the rates of obesity, prevent chronic diseases, and cut health care costs over time. It is a community's problem and requires a community's solution. In order for children and families to make healthy choices, there must be policies in place in their environments that support healthy living. The socio-ecological model of public health shows that change occurring across all levels, from individuals to organizations and institutions, and blanketed in policy change, is sustainable change.

The mission of TKF, in partnership with community members, is to prevent and reduce childhood obesity by empowering local children and families to eat healthy and be active. The working groups include: health care, school systems, childcare and preschool providers, governmental policies and programs, community based organizations and faith groups, businesses, and work sites.

## Goals:

- Foster and promote partnerships within the community
- Lower obesity rates in local children
- Achieve measurable improvements in nutrition and physical activity in all local children
- Increase access to healthy foods and physical activity opportunities for all children and families
- Advocate for policy change in support of these goals
- Ensure that children of all cultures and socioeconomic backgrounds are included in our mission

## 2. Programs

*Since its inception, TKF has worked to form partnerships; support and advocate for existing groups in the community; and focus in the areas where there will be sustainable change and the greatest impact. TKF has received grant funding from the Community Health Endowment to work on school policy reform in local public schools. TKF works with the Alliance for a Healthier Generation, a national organization organized to reduce the nationwide prevalence of childhood obesity by 2015 and to empower kids nationwide to make healthy lifestyle choices. TKF also recently hosted "Healthy Students are Smart Students", a forum for principals and wellness advocates from LPS. As a result, to date, 30 public schools have signed on as partners with the Alliance for a Healthier Generation. These schools are starting to work toward incorporating best practice wellness strategies into their buildings. LPS was recently announced as a recipient of a U.S. Dept. of Education PEP (Physical Education Program) grant. The 17 elementary schools with Community Learning Centers will start to work on incorporating evidence-based physical education, physical activity, and nutrition programming over the next 3 years. TKF is the community-based organization offering our in-kind support to LPS on the PEP grant. The Nebraska Medical Association Foundation has funded TKF to start the Physicians for a Healthy Nebraska Childhood Obesity Prevention Project, which will provide education, resources, outreach, and policy/advocacy support to physicians. TKF has also received a grant from NE DHHS for the development of physician toolkits, a webinar, and patient education office resources. We are also collaborating with the LLCHD on a 54321Go! social marketing campaign.*

*Different groups in our community have focused on the issue of childhood obesity, but not in a comprehensive coordinated way — until TKF. Dr. _____, a pediatrician in town, had taken on childhood obesity as a priority in her practice, but in order to serve her patients, the children and families in the community determined that a public health initiative was warranted. The services in the town had been fragmented, and health care providers had not taken a leading role. Dr. _____, a family practitioner and faculty at the Medical Education Partnership, saw the byproducts of this epidemic in his young adult patients. In order to have the greatest impact, Dr. _____ decided to pursue his MPH degree, and is leading the school systems working group and data surveillance. We are bringing together organizations and community members to work on a shared mission to stand at a level of commitment to this important cause.*

# Resources

This is by no means an exhaustive list of resources. Your area of endeavor will determine many of the resources that you may require or that may be of value to you. Included here are general resources for grant seeking and grant writing. Some of these resources are repeated from the summary of Section 2.

The Foundation Center
**http://foundationcenter.org/**

The Foundation Center is recognized as the nation's leading center on organized philanthropy. The tools of the Foundation Center are geared toward grant seekers, grant makers, researchers, policy makers, the media, and the general public. If there ever was a prime place to start to learn about the greater world of philanthropy, this is it.

Foundation Grants to Individuals Online
**http://gtionline.foundationcenter.org/**

This Web site is connected to the Foundation Center, but it is important to mention this resource separately, as it caters — as the name implies — to individual grant seekers. This is a subscription service that has descriptions of nearly 8,000 foundation programs that provide funding to students, artists, researchers, and other individuals looking for funding. As it is often quite difficult for individuals to locate foundations that fund projects not associated with 501(c) (3) organizations, this is a unique resource.

## The Chronicle of Philanthropy

**http://philanthropy.com/**

*The Chronicle of Philanthropy* is "The Newspaper of the Nonprofit World." Their Web site and newspaper contains a great deal of valuable and up-to-date information. Their Web site features a guide to grants, a nonprofit handbook, and other information that will keep you well-informed on managing and raising funds for nonprofit organizations.

## Association of Small Foundations

**www.smallfoundations.org**

This is an organization that is not aimed at the grant seeker but at the small philanthropic foundations with little or no staff. There are about 3,000 members of this association. This site is useful because it helps gain the point of view of these small foundations. Information that can be found here includes foundation strategies for tough economic times, lists of association members by state, and a variety of publications that help in getting the small foundation perspective on philanthropy.

## FoundationSearch

**www.foundationsearch.com**

FoundationSearch is a source of fundraising information aimed specifically at nonprofit organizations. Their Web site includes more than 120,000 foundations that grant billions of dollars annually. FoundationSearch provides its members with tools to locate grants in a variety of ways.

The Philanthropy Journal

**www.philanthropyjournal.org**

The Journal's Web site provides nonprofit news and resource tools that are valuable to those researching and seeking foundation grants.

GuideStar

**www.guidestar.org**

GuideStar collects and disseminates information about nonprofit organizations. They have a huge database that includes mission statements, strategic plans, lists of directors, priorities... and it is free. It is a valuable, trusted resource.

Innovation Network

**www.innonet.org**

This is a great resource when you are in the planning or assessment mode. Innovation Network provides tools to nonprofits to strategize and plan for the long and short term

The Proposal Writer

**www.proposalwriter.com/grants.html**

The link provided here is to the Web site of Deborah Kluge, and her site's link page is a great resource of other resources. The resources offered by this Web site are about as exhaustive as you may find on the Internet, providing links to everything from community foundation locators, to open directories of grant-making organizations, to state foundation directories.

There are countless resources available in more specified areas. Whether you are searching for funding in the arts, conservation, education, energy, religion, or youth programming, there is likely a Web site that can guide you on your path. Most of the resources listed above will probably be able to get you started in the right direction.

You may be able to find some useful information at your city library, but be careful about relying too heavily on foundation directories you might find at the library, as they can be outdated. If you find a foundation directory at your library, make sure it has been published within the last year — two at the most. Any foundation listing you get from any source, whether in a published book or from a Web site, should be followed-up with a phone call to check how accurate the information is.

# Bibliography

Brown, Larissa Golden & Brown, Martin John. *Demystifying Grant Seeking*. San Francisco, CA, Jossey-Bass, 2001.

Browning, Beverly. *Grant Writing for Dummies*. New Jersey, Wiley Publishing, 2009.

Carlson, Mim & O'Neal-McElrath, Tori. *Winning Grants*. San Francisco, CA, Jossey-Bass, 2008.

Foundation Center. *Guide to Proposal Writing*. Washington, D.C., Foundation Center, 2007.

Freund, Gerald. *Narcissism and Philanthropy*. New York, NY, Viking Penguin, 1996.

Kuniholm, Roland. *The Complete Book of Model Fund-Raising Letters*. Englewood Cliffs, NJ, Prentice-Hall, 1995.

Wason, Sarah Deming. *Webster's New World Grant Writing Handbook*. New York, Wiley Publishing, 2004.

# Author Biography

Richard Helweg has more than 25 years' experience working in the nonprofit sector as an artistic Director, managing director, and executive director. He is an award-winning playwright and has recently written *...And Justice for All: A History of the Supreme Court*, a book for young readers. Richard lives in Lincoln, Nebraska, with his wife, Karen, and sons Aedan and Rory.

# Index